Treasure From the
Haunted Pagoda

The Haunted Pagoda

Treasure From the

HAUNTED PAGODA

By
ERIC B. HARE

Illustrated by Vernon Nye

Pacific Press Publishing Association
Boise, Idaho
Montemorelos, Nuevo Leon, Mexico
Oshawa, Ontario, Canada

Cover design by Ichiro Nakashima

ISBN 0-8163-0586-2

85 86 87 88 89 • 6 5 4 3 2 1

Dedicated
to
The YOUNG PEOPLE OF CALIFOR-
NIA, *whose bright faces and big eyes
around the glowing campfires inspired me
to put this story together. And also to Mr.
Fred Sampson, beloved Junior camp cook
and "General Sound Effects," who helped
to make the story very real.*

Contents

Foreword

YEARS and years ago a little five-year-old boy knelt at his mother's knee and repeated this little prayer, phrase by phrase, after her. "And, dear Lord, when I grow up, may I be a missionary—at the four corners of the earth—preaching the gospel—for Jesus' sake. Amen."

This story, *Treasure From the Haunted Pagoda*, tells the marvelous way in which God prepared the "special place," where that little boy, when he grew to manhood, could serve Him best. It is true from beginning to end, and even the superstitious tales of the devil worshipers are narrated as nearly as possible, word for word, the way they were told. Throughout these pages you can trace again and again the blow for blow given by the forces of evil and the forces of righteousness in the great Christian battle, the controversy between Christ and Satan.

ERIC B. HARE.

The Haunted Pagoda at Ohn Daw

><><><><><><><><

"The Lord thy God, He will go over before thee, and He will destroy these nations from before thee, and thou shalt possess them." Deuteronomy 31:3.

Just Then We Heard a Low, Grumbling, Growling Sound. My Hair
Stood on End

CHAPTER 1

The Haunted Pagoda
at Ohn Daw

><-><-><-><-><-><-><-><

YEARS AND YEARS and years ago, when our grand-
parents were just boys and girls, after the troublous wars
of 1824, when the English took Lower Burma, there was
a great deal of movement among the tribespeople of interior
Burma as they readjusted themselves to their new condi-
tions. No longer afraid of the aggressive Burmese, a tribe
of Talaings traveling westward from the northern hills of
Siam came to the eastern bank of the great Salween River,
and there built themselves a village. At this place thirty-
three little hills rose abruptly from the riverbank, and on
the top of every hill the Talaings built a tiny brick pagoda.
Circular, whitewashed, with a footprint of Buddha carved
in marble and encased in a shrine of solid silver bricks hidden deep in the foundations, and tipped with a crown of
brass bells, each pagoda lent oriental beauty to the village,
and as the evening winds blew, sweet tinkling music
sounded everywhere. They named the place The Village
of Thirty-Three Pagodas.

Shortly after this, on the opposite bank of the river, a tribe of Shans traveling south from the Shan Hills of Burma built themselves a village. There were no hills on that side of the river on which to build pagodas, but because the land was excellent for rice cultivation and gardens, they planted coconut palms in order to make their village beautiful, and as the years went by, the tufty tops of the coconut palms waved softly in the evening breeze, adding beauty and elegance to this village and giving it the name Ohn Daw, meaning "The Cluster of Palms."

Before long friendly competition sprang up between the young men of these two villages. They competed in racing canoes on the river; they competed with elephants dragging logs in the forest; they competed at building bamboo houses. But with this competition there grew a spirit of jealousy and envy and hatred in the hearts of these people, until at last the Talaings said to the Shans, "Don't you dare to cross over the river into our village. If you do we will kill you."

And the Shans retaliated with, "If you dare show your dirty faces in our village, we will chop your heads off." So they hated each other, and hated each other all the more as the years went by.

Then one day, when the babies of Ohn Daw had grown to men and women, there came a terrible flood. The river rose its usual thirty-five feet, and then five feet more, overflowing its banks and spreading mud and water for miles and miles on either side. The rice fields of the Shan people were covered with water.

"What shall we do? Oh, what shall we do?" cried the old men as they assembled in council.

"Doesn't anyone know another place where the evil

12

spirits live where we might sacrifice another pig or another chicken? We have sacrificed at every known place, and still the flood continues. A few more days and our rice will be destroyed and famine must be our lot."

Here and there throughout the forest, in front of clumps of bamboo and strange-looking rocks, sacrifices were offered, but to no avail. The flood continued for three weeks. The rice of the Shan people was destroyed, and famine came to them that year.

"Let's get out of here," said the old men. "Let's get out of here while the getting out is good. Can't you see that there is an evil spirit in this place whom we do not know, who will not be appeased by our many offerings?"

But the young men said, "Grandfathers and elders, don't go so quickly. Look at this beautiful village. Look at these beautiful palm trees. Think of the number of years we have lived here without any flood. Can't you see this is only chance, and it comes to one and all in the course of a life-time? Let's not leave this beautiful village, but rather next year let us plant our rice a little earlier; then if the flood comes again it will be high enough to poke out above the water, and thus save us from another famine."

The arguments of the young men prevailed over the counsel of the old men, and they stayed another year.

But the next year there came another flood. Higher than ever the waters rose, and famine came to the Shan village for the second year in succession.

"Let's get out of here. Let's get out of here," urged the old men again. "Let's get out of here while the getting out is good, for now we know that there is an evil spirit living in this forest whom we do not know and to whom we cannot sacrifice. Let's get out before we are all dead."

13

But the young men said, "Don't go too quickly. Look, yonder village of Thirty-Three Pagodas has had good rice for two years, while we have had famine. They have had plenty, while we have been in want. They have thirty-three pagodas, and we have none. Can't you see? Can't you see? That is why bad luck has come to us these two years running. Instead of moving away, let's build ourselves a pagoda, and perhaps fortune will smile upon us, so that our crops will be plentiful again.

Again the arguments of the young men prevailed over the counsel of the old men, and they stayed another year.

The young men went to the rice fields and puddled mud to make bricks. The marble footprint of Buddha within its little room of silver bricks was secretely concealed, and then the old men rolled great rocks together near the riverbank to form the foundation for their pagoda. The women and the girls, with baskets full of dirt, filled in between the cracks of the great boulders. The bricks were burned, and layer by layer the pagoda was built on the top of its rocky foundation. Circular, symmetrical, and beautiful, it rose, and was at last finished and whitewashed all over.

Then they sought out a cunning workman to make a crown of brass bells, and at the full of the moon their heralds went to all the near-by villages to call them to the feast of the dedication of the pagoda at Ohn Daw.

There was great excitement in the jungle that day. Crowds and crowds came, with their clarinets made of bamboo, their brass cymbals, their rawhide drums, their tinkling bells, their dancing costumes, and accompanied by their yellow-robed Buddhist priests. They came to dance, to eat, to drink and be merry, and after the night's festivity, while the moon was at the full, the pagoda would be crowned with its brass bells, and then success and happiness would surely come to the Shan village.

But that night, during the festivities, a terrible storm arose. The thunder roared, the lightning flashed, the winds howled, the rain came down, and in the morning the little pagoda was found with its top broken right off.

"There you are," said the old men. "We told you. We told you. We cannot live here. There is an evil spirit. Come on; let us go. Let's go."

But the young men said, "Wait a minute, grandfathers and elders, don't let us go too quickly. Look at these beautiful palm trees. Look at this beautiful village. Look at our beautiful rice fields. Can't you see that a thunder storm is likely to come at any time? It is only chance that breaks our pagoda. Nay, nay, let us not go, but we shall postpone the crowning of our pagoda for one moon, and then we shall crown it successfully and live here happily forever after."

So they stayed another month, and during the month the young men went to Moulmein and bought cement to mix with their mortar, and by the full of the next moon it was all repaired and whitewashed again and once more ready to be crowned.

Once more the dancers and singers and musicians came with their instruments and fancy clothes and their yellow-robed priests. Once more they enjoyed a night of dancing and revelry, and were sure that the next morning they would crown their pagoda with the brass bells.

But that night there came another terrible storm. The thunder roared, the lightning flashed, the winds howled, and the rains came down, and in the morning the pagoda was found broken down for the second time.

"Come on. Come on," cried the old men, "Let's go. Let's go. What further proof do you need that this place is cursed with evil spirits too powerful to be found, too powerful to be worshiped? Come, let's go before we are all dead men!"

But the young men said, "Nay, nay; not yet. We will try once more to crown our pagoda successfully, for we cannot tell if it be a curse unless it happens three times. So we shall postpone our festivity for one more month and try yet again." And they added in a whisper, "If it happens the third time, you will not have to tell us to go any more. We will be gone before you get up in the morning."

During the next month so determined were the young men to crown their pagoda successfully that they dug a hole down the center of the pagoda and placed a green post cut from a near-by tree in it. Then around the post they built their bricks until their pagoda was all repaired and ready to be crowned once more.

Eagerly the crowds waited for the full of the moon, and then again they assembled with their musical instruments and costumes and their priests. Again they enjoyed a night of festivity, planning to crown the pagoda the next morning. But that night there arose another storm, more terrible than any before. The thunder roared, the lightning flashed, the winds howled, and the rains fell. Some say that even the earth shook, and the next morning the pagoda was broken down for the third time.

"Let's go. Let's go," cried the old men. "Let's go, while the going is good."

But the young men were too busy to reply. They were tying their pigs' legs together so that they could carry them away on bamboo poles. They were putting their rice into their blankets and tying each end so that they could carry

16

them easily. Little babies were tied to the backs of their mothers. The chickens were caught and put into baskets, and then, with their bullock wagons loaded to capacity, with everyone carrying some kind of load, the Shan people of Ohn Daw left their village in fear and terror.

Before the old men left they called together the Buddhist priests and said, "Curse for us this pagoda. Curse for us this place of worship. If we cannot live here we do not want anyone else to live here either."

So, lighting candles and placing them around the broken pagoda, the priests walked around it, intoning the curse:

> "Cursed be this pagoda.
> Cursed be this place of worship.
> May it be only the abode of devils.
> May it be only inhabited by evil spirits.
> Cursed be they that worship here,
> And cursed be any who try to take the treasure
>   from its foundations.
> May they perish in the attempt."

Thus the old men left, and scattered into the near-by villages, afraid to live in Ohn Daw—beautiful Ohn Daw, the Village of Palm Trees—any longer, and they say that at night you could hear the most horrible sounds from the old cursed pagoda.

Soon after this, war again broke out, and in 1885, when the English annexed Upper Burma, news of the terrible guns and cannons that the white men carried again brought unrest to the tribespeople of the interior. Across the river, in the village of Thirty-Three Pagodas, the Talaing elders met in council.

"Let's move away from here," they said. "We are too

2   17

close to this great river. Let's move away from this place lest the white men come here too with their thunder sticks and their lightning sticks and kill us all."

With solemn ceremony the headman took a diamond and, going to the spirit tree on the side of the hill, with no one present, made an incision in the bark, buried his diamond deep in the heart of the tree, and then chanted this prayer:

> "Oh, Spirit of the Forest,
> Spirit of the Mountains,
> We have lived here for many years in comfort
>   and in plenty,
> But now we are going away.
> Since we cannot live here for fear of guns and
>   cannons,
> We do not want anyone else to live here either.
> So we are implanting in your heart an ever-
>   lasting offering.
> As long as this diamond shall be embedded in
>   thy heart,
> Watch over this place and keep it for us,
> If ever we come back again.
> Curse anyone who shall try to build a village
>   here.
> Curse anyone that tries to steal this everlasting
>   offering from thy heart.
> Yea, curse him with sudden death."

Then the Talaings dug up their silver bricks from the foundations of their thirty-three pagodas, loaded the treasure onto the backs of eight elephants, and, with their families and pigs and chickens, went seven days' journey back into the hills of Siam and built themselves another village there.

So the two once-prosperous villages on the banks of the mighty Salween River were now left desolate.

Years and years went by. Year by year the torrential rains came down. Little by little the bamboo houses rotted and fell into decay. Little by little the jungle creepers grew, until, except for the tufty tops of the coconut palms that still lifted their hands heavenward above the tangle of jungle growth, you might never know there had been a village there.

Then one day there came a hunter with his dog by his side and with his gun on his shoulder. He was chasing a deer through the forest when suddenly before him there loomed a little hill.

"Well," he said, "what's this? It's not big enough for a hill. Looks as though it has been built here."

Going a little closer, he pulled aside the little trees and jungle creepers and saw the broken brick remains of a pagoda.

"A pagoda! A pagoda!" he cried. "This must be the cursed Pagoda of Ohn Daw, and there is treasure at the bottom of it! When I get to the village tonight, I must ask the headman if anyone has ever dug for the silver bricks."

That night when he got to the village he said to the headman, "Today while I was hunting I came upon the old Pagoda of Ohn Daw. Tell me—has anyone ever tried to dig the treasure?"

Lowering his voice to a whisper, the headman raised a warning finger and said, "Haven't you heard? Don't you know? Hasn't anyone ever told you? The place is cursed. The treasure is cursed. The one who takes it shall perish in the attempt." Then he told him of the two years of famine and the three unsuccessful attempts to crown the pagoda.

"Ha! ha! ha!" laughed the hunter, "but I am not afraid of curses. Look, I am tattooed with medicine from my head

19

to my feet. While it might be fatal to others, no harm shall come to me."

So he took a hoe and a basket, and he went to the old cursed pagoda. Clearing away the jungle from one side, he began to tunnel into its foundations. Deeper and deeper he dug; nearer and nearer to the treasure he came. Then one day the hole caved in on him and killed him.

When he did not turn up at the village at evening, his friends went to find him, and brought back his body. Fear seized upon everybody. The news spread far and wide. Nobody dared go anywhere near, and they say that at night weird screams and yells came from the offended spirits that were guarding the treasure. They say that at certain times a ball of fire would come out of that hole, ascend into the air, circle the pagoda, and go back again to the treasure. People feared to mention the name of Ohn Daw. It was whispered around the campfires at night as we whisper when we tell ghost stories. The road between the near-by villages was moved a quarter of a mile farther away from the pagoda so that innocent travelers would not even have to look at the cursed haunted place.

A few more years went by, and then one day there came to the spot another hunter. He had a dog by his side and a gun on his shoulder, and, as he was hunting through the forest, pursuing a deer, he came to the almost-forgotten mound hidden in the tangled jungle creepers. As he neared it he paused for breath, and through the creepers he saw broken bricks.

"Oh! oh! oh!" he said, "an old pagoda!"

He drew nearer, pulled apart the creepers, and gazed upon the ruin. There before him was the hole.

"Someone has been digging," he said to himself. "I

20

wonder how much treasure he got. I must ask the headman when I get to the village tonight."

And that night he said excitedly to the headman, "Tell me, How much treasure did the man get who dug the hole in the old pagoda?"

The headman looked cautiously around, lowered his voice to a whisper, raised his finger in an attitude of warning, and then whispered, "Don't you know? Haven't you heard? Didn't anybody ever tell you?" Then he told him the story of the two years of famine, the three attempts to crown the pagoda, and the death of the first man who dared to defy the curse of the Ohn Daw pagoda.

"Ha, ha, ha!" laughed the second hunter. "He wasn't tattooed with the right kind of medicine. But I am. Look on my chest, on my back, on my arms, on my legs. I am magic-proof, and curseproof, bulletproof, and knifeproof. Though he was killed before he reached the treasure, I will get it. Never fear. Watch me."

Then he took his hoe and his basket, and went to the pagoda. He got into the hole the first hunter had dug, took out the bricks that had fallen in, and then worked carefully, digging deeper and deeper, getting nearer and nearer to the treasure.

But one day the hole caved in on top of him, and he was so badly hurt that he could only crawl home, and just as he entered the village he died.

After that, people even feared to call the name of that cursed place, and travelers brought weirder and weirder stories of terrible groans and screams that issued forth from the place that had now claimed two victims, and no more attempts were made to wrest from the foundation of the pagoda its buried treasure.

21

Years and years went by, until in 1915 Elder Heber Votaw, who was then the superintendent of our mission in Burma, called his mission committee together.

"Brethren," he said, "I have a burden on my heart today for the Karen devil worshipers of this land. I have been reading of the great success that has come to other missionaries who have labored among those that worship the evil spirits. It almost seems that it is easier for them to accept the gospel than it is for these complacent Buddhists, and I propose that we select two men of our committee and give them authority to go into the heart of the Karen country and try to find a suitable site for our mission station."

The result of that meeting was that Elder George A. Hamilton and Elder A. H. Williams were commissioned to travel up the Salween River in search of a mission station among the devil worshipers.

To old Moulmein they went by train; then after hiring a big canoe and some men to row it, they started upstream. Day by day they traveled, looking for a site for the mission station. Day by day they examined land to the right and to the left, but always they were disappointed to find that the places that were suitable for mission stations were already occupied by Buddhist temples or villages, and the places that were not occupied were either unhealthy or too rocky for cultivation. Thus for five days they journeyed on, rowing, toiling, searching, until at last, weary and disappointed, they almost gave up hope of ever finding anything within reach of the outside world and still within the territory of the devil worshipers.

But that evening, right ahead of them, Elder Williams saw a beautiful cluster of coconut palms.

"Say, look at that, Brother Hamilton," he cried. "Doesn't

22

that cluster of palms look cool and inviting? Let's make our camp there tonight." And within half an hour their canoe was pulled up on the riverbank and tied to the foot of one of the old coconut palms in the deserted village of Ohn Daw.

They made their camp there that night, and the next morning, while Elder Williams was preparing breakfast, Elder Hamilton walked up and down the bank of the river. To the north he could see for two and a half miles as the great Salween River gushed forth from one of the most marvelous mountain canyons that geographers have ever known. To the south he could see for eight miles as that mighty river, half a mile wide, ribboned its way in and out of the extensive rice fields.

"Say, Williams," he cried, "this would be an ideal place for a mission station. Look at that wonderful river. Look at those marvelous mountains. Let's hurry up with breakfast, and as soon as it is over let's go to the village headman and see if we can buy this piece of land."

After breakfast they went to the nearest village and, entering the headman's house, sat down and said, "Mr. Headman, last night we made our camp up near the old coconut palms. We would like to know who owns that piece of land, for we are anxious to establish a mission station up here somewhere, and we feel that if the price is not too high we should like to buy that site for our mission station."

The old headman leaned forward, lowered his voice to a whisper, and, lifting his finger in an attitude of warning, said, "Don't you know? Haven't you heard? Hasn't anybody ever told you?" and he then told Elder Hamilton and Elder Williams the story I have just told you, the story of the jealous villages and the two years of famine, the story of the cursed pagoda and the buried treasure, and of the death of the two daring hunters. Then he added, "You had better not build a mission station there. You could not live there in the first place, and in the second place you could not get anyone from this part of the world to go to a school or a hospital that you might build at Ohn Daw."

Then Mr. Hamilton laughed. "Ha, ha, ha! Mr. Headman, we are not afraid of curses or evil spirits. We worship a God who is stronger than all the forces of evil, and something seems to tell me that God wants us to build a mission station in that place. Will you give me the address of the nearest government official? I would like to write to him to see if we could obtain the old village site for a mission station."

The letter was written, and in just three weeks' time he received a reply. It read something like this:

"DEAR MR. HAMILTON: You are hereby granted, free from all taxes, for mission purposes, the old village site of Ohn Daw—The Cluster of Palm Trees."

The letter was signed by the district commissioner at Papun.

With all speed Elder Hamilton and his wife and two little boys, Edward and Sydney, with Miss Mary Gibbs, who was to be the dispensary nurse, moved onto the place. A little clearing was made in the dense jungle. A mat house was erected. Coolies were hired to clear the land. Elephants began to drag in logs. Carpenters moved in to build the mission bungalow and dispensary, and just then Mrs. Hare and I arrived in Burma to be the associate missionaries of Elder and Mrs. Hamilton on their mission station among the devil worshipers.

24

"Come up with me, Brother Hare," said Elder Hamilton, as he met us at the boat. "We want to get our land ready for the government surveyor, and I need you to help me get our pegs ready and to cut the line which shall form the boundary of our mission property."

So Mrs. Hare and I went up for a visit, and during our visit Elder Hamilton and I began clearing our border lines. From the river we cut inland until our survey peg was right beside the road. Then skirting the road northward, we went until we felt that we had encompassed a piece of land of about seven acres. Then we turned eastward and cut our boundary line down to the river's edge again. As we cut, suddenly there loomed up before us a jungle-covered mound.

"Elder Hamilton, what's this?" I said. We moved closer with our brush hooks, tore away some of the tangled creepers, and found broken bricks. Our eyes bulged a little. "It is the old haunted pagoda, Brother Hamilton," I said. "Are you scared?"

"No, come on, let's climb up on it," he replied.

Up over the rocks of the foundation we climbed, cutting and clearing the tall grass and the creepers and the little trees as we went. There before our eyes we beheld a great tree growing out of the very top of it. It was the post that the young men had embedded in the heart of the pagoda years and years before. Now it had grown roots and branches, and waved its long arms from the top of the broken ruins. Right into the foundation was the hole where two hunters had lost their lives digging for the buried treasure. Down into the hole we jumped. We felt a long way from everywhere. I looked at Brother Hamilton, and he looked at me.

"Let's dig for the treasure, Brother Hamilton," I said.
"Very well, Brother Hare, let's do," he replied. But further speech became suddenly impossible, for just then we heard a low grumbling, growling sound, which increased in volume for a second or two till it ended in a dull thud at our very feet.

2

Preparing to Dig

✕✕✕✕✕✕✕✕✕✕

"If thou seekest her as silver, and searchest for her as for hid treasures; then shalt thou understand the fear of the Lord, and find the knowledge of God." Proverbs 2:4, 5.

"Fine! Fine! Fine! Now Please Tell Ma Ma to Dance for Us"

Preparing to Dig

>+>+>+>+>+>+>+>+>+

M Y HAIR STOOD ON END! My eyes bulged!
For a second I looked at my feet to see if the ball of fire was
going to come out of the ground. Then all of a sudden I
breathed easily, for there at our feet was half of a brick that
had rumbled innocently down the side of the hole. We
laughed while we blinked our eyes back in and stroked
our hair back down, and then Elder Hamilton said, "They
say there's treasure under the old haunted pagoda. What
do you say, Thara? Shall we dig for the treasure?"

We looked into each other's eyes for just a moment,
reading each other's thoughts, and then I said, "Of course
we'll dig; we'll dig for the treasure—treasure that's more
valuable than silver or gold or rubies or diamonds. But
we'll need more than baskets and hoes for our work, so I
must first go to Rangoon to study the language of the people who dwell in the land of the haunted pagoda."

For the next six months Mrs. Hare and I studied the Karen language for all we were worth. We had read in the *Encyclopaedia Britannica* that the Karen language was monosyllabic, and had expected therefore to find something easy, but we soon found where the catch was. Since there were not enough syllables for all the words, to each syllable had been given six tones—high, low, descending, short high, short low, and singsong—so that one single syllable could mean six or more different things, and to our dismay we discovered it was very easy for us to get the tones mixed up and say the wrong thing in the right place. For instance, take the syllable *ler*, the high tone means "by, from, or at"; the low tone means "stone"; the descending, "maggot"; the high short, "all"; the low short, "use up"; and the singsong tone means "warm." You can see what horrible possibilities a mistake in the tones could produce.

We had been studying about six weeks when our teacher said one day, "Mr. Hare, you are certainly getting along splendidly." We thought we were too. Then he added, "Won't you come down to my home and spend the evening? My big son is home from college. He plays the piano very well, and we will have a pleasant time."

I wanted to say, "We shall be very pleased to come, and I will bring my silver-plated trumpet with me and play on it for you," but I got my tones mixed up, and what I actually said was, "We shall be very pleased to come, and I will bring my silver-plated grandmother with me and play on it for you."

"Oh, Mr. Hare, Mr. Hare," exclaimed our teacher. "You can't play on your grandmother."

"Oh, but let me show you," I insisted and soon had my trumpet on exhibition.

"Oh, Mr. Hare, Mr. Hare," he groaned, "that's not a *Be* (high), that's a *Be* (descending)," and I had to learn that there was all the world of difference between a *Be* (high) and a *Be* (descending). The only consolation seemed to be that we were not the only ones to get our tones mixed up. Miss Gibbs, the dispensary nurse, one day horrified a jungle mother by asking for a little "hell" to wash the baby in. Of course, she meant a basin, but there wasn't nearly so much difference in the *sound* of the words as there was in the *things* themselves. My associate missionary of later years, Mr. Baird, when announcing the opening hymn the first time he acted as Sabbath school superintendent, invited the congregation to "please stand up and starve." Of course, they didn't starve, but they could hardly sing for smiling.

There were other things to worry about in addition to the tones—the peculiar way they had of saying things. For "What is your name?" they say, "Your name how?" When you put on your shoes you "ride your shoes." When you receive your wages you "eat" them, you "drink" smoke, if you smoke tobacco, and fever "eats" you if you are sick. However, after about six months the day came when, with a good start in our book knowledge of the language, we moved up to the Karen mission station at Ohn Daw, where we assisted Elder G. A. Hamilton and Miss Gibbs in the dispensary while continuing the study of our language in a practical way through daily association with the people we were to serve.

How good it was to have the association of our senior missionaries for the next two years, for, although we were thrilled with the assurance that God had marvelously brought us to this place to find treasure, we were also dismayed with our own need of better tools and better training for the task that lay before us.

"Thara, I've got a tooth that I want to get pulled out," said a jungle man as he came up the steps to the dispensary one day while I was relieving Nurse Gibbs, who was out on a call. I suddenly realized that my nurses' course had not included dentistry, but I couldn't send him home again; so I told him to sit down, and then tried to paint around the loose tooth with oil of cloves. How that swab shook and trembled. I thought it might be my nervousness, so I said, "Mr. Hare! Control yourself! Control yourself!" But it did no good. As I picked up the forceps, they shook and trembled so much that it was with the greatest difficulty that I finally got them fastened on that tooth, and I must confess that that first tooth really fell out with the vibrations.

The patient himself was happy enough as he went home, but I couldn't help thinking, "Mr. Hare, you must learn to be a better dentist and a doctor too."

"Better come with me to visit some of the villages on the other side of the river," said Nurse Gibbs one day. Mrs. Hare and I were delighted to break away from our study for a few hours, so away we went. But, as we neared the first village in our little motor launch, we caught a glimpse of one or two startled faces and heard the cry *"Dawtaka! Dawtaka!"* Then by the screaming and dog barking that followed we knew they were running away for dear life.

"What does *dawtaka* mean, Miss Gibbs?" I asked as we entered the empty village.

"A *dawtaka* is a half-breed between a devil and a ghost," she replied, "and it is supposed to have the power to steal away the babies. Then it *feeds* them up, *fattens* them up, and then *eats* them up!"

32

No wonder they ran away! No wonder they screamed! And as we came home, I said, "Mr. Hare, you will never find treasure till you've found a way to take the fear from the hearts of the jungle people." So we set our hearts with a will to the task of preparing for the work that lay ahead.

The year following, Elder Hamilton was called to work in Rangoon, and the responsibility of the Karen mission station fell on our shoulders.

"What shall we do?" I said to my good wife as we studied our problem.

"Why not start a Sabbath school?" she said. "Then, as they come to Sabbath school, we will be able to give them Bible studies, and little by little we will have them ready for baptism; then we can organize a church."

Nurse Gibbs also said that was the way to do it, and I said, "Fine! Fine!" That week I visited all the villages within ten miles of us and told the people, "We're going to have Sabbath school at the mission station next Sabbath morning at nine o'clock. Be sure to come, and we will sing you nice songs, show you beautiful pictures, and tell you lovely stories."

"Ugh, ugh," they grunted in assent.

With much anticipation, next Sabbath morning Mrs. Hare and I got ready for Sabbath school. We put some bamboo mats on the floor for the people to sit on, hung the Picture Roll on the wall, put up the folding organ, and with my trumpet all ready to play I walked up and down on the veranda, waiting for the people to come. We waited and waited and waited. All day long we waited, but nobody came. Finally I said to Mrs. Hare, "Well, now what are we going to do?"

"Well," she said, "we mustn't get discouraged just because they didn't come the first day. Maybe they forgot, and maybe they will come next week."

Accordingly, the next week I went around to the same villages again, and I said, "We missed you at Sabbath school last Sabbath."

"Oh, yes," they replied. "We forgot. We forgot."

"Well, be sure to come next Sabbath," I begged, "and we'll sing you nice songs and show you beautiful pictures and tell you lovely stories."

"Ugh! Ugh! Sure! Sure!" they grunted in chorus till I just knew they would come this time. So next Sabbath morning we got ready for Sabbath school again. We put the bamboo mats on the floor for the people to sit on, hung the Picture Roll on the wall, put up the folding organ, and, with my trumpet all ready to play again, I walked up and down on the veranda, waiting for the people to come. But we waited and waited and waited and waited all day long, and still nobody came. Nobody came the next week or the next week or the next or the next. For six weeks nobody came. And then one Sabbath morning before I was dressed I heard someone calling from across the river. "Oh, Thara! Oh, Thara!"

I jumped out of bed and ran out onto the veranda, and there across the river I could see two hundred of them dressed in their best clothes—all coming to Sabbath school. I called Mrs. Hare to see the glorious sight. "Here they come, my dear," I called. "It takes some time for them to get the idea, but now look at them!"

I then ran downstairs, picked up an oar, called a man to follow me, and rowed across the river in our big canoe to bring the wonderful crowd to Sabbath school.

"I'm so glad you've come to Sabbath school at last," I

said to the first old man who stepped in, as the canoe grounded on the sandbank on the opposite shore of the river.

He said, "Ugh?"

I repeated, "I'm so glad you've come to Sabbath school at last."

He said, "Ugh? Sabbath school? What's that?"

I said, "The nice songs we are going to sing to you, the beautiful pictures we are going to show you, and the lovely stories we are going ———"

"Oh, Sabbath school," he broke in. "Why, we're not coming to Sabbath school."

"Then wherever on earth are you going all dressed up like this if you're not going to Sabbath school?" I asked, and he replied, "Don't you know? Haven't you heard? Hasn't anyone ever told you? At the village three miles beyond your house they are having a big devil dance today, and we are all going to the devil dance!"

Did I feel sick! All the rest of that day I sat "astonished." At last I turned to my good wife and asked, "Well, what are we going to do now?"

She was thoughtful for a moment, then replied, "Well, if they won't come to the Sabbath school, why don't we take the Sabbath school to them?"

"Excellent idea," I replied. "That's just exactly what we'll do."

So the next Sabbath, with my trumpet, the Picture Roll, and a bag of medicines for the sick folks, we started off to have Sabbath school in the nearest village. It was just across the river, about two miles away, and as we entered it we noticed two huge tiger skins drying in the sun. We began visiting the sick ones and as we administered their fever mixture, treated their sore eyes, or put ointment on their sores, we always said, "When you hear the music in the headman's house, be sure to come and we'll sing you nice songs and show you beautiful pictures and tell you lovely stories," and, when at last the music started, they surely did come. So many came that we had to come down from the house and have our Sabbath school outside for fear the house would break down. They crowded around—mothers, fathers, aunties, uncles, nieces, nephews, grandfathers, and grandmothers—and, when I stopped for breath, they clapped their hands and cried, "Fine! Fine! Oh, that was fine! Now sing for us!"

How happy I was, for that was just what I wanted. You see, it is rather hard to begin abruptly to preach a sermon to people who have no idea of what a religious service is, but when you have sung a hymn you simply ask, "Did you understand the words?" and when they say "No," you say, "Then I'll explain them to you," and as you explain the words you preach your sermon.

So with joyful hearts we sang. We sang two hymns, and I was just reaching for the Picture Roll and clearing my voice to say, "Did you understand the words?" when they broke out into applause again, and as they clapped their hands they cried, "Fine! Fine! Fine! Now please tell Ma Ma to dance for us!"

It might sound funny to you, but it didn't sound funny to us. We had gone to have Sabbath school, and for a second or two we didn't know what to do about the dancing. But God gave us something to say, and in a few moments they were listening intently to the Sabbath school story.

You can only imagine how thrilled we were when we reached home that evening to realize that we had actually held a Sabbath school among the superstitious devil wor-shipers. By faith we looked forward to the time when many such Sabbath schools would be organized and many of the jungle people would become God's peculiar treasure. As the four of us continued to meet in our own little Sabbath school at the mission station, Nurse Gibbs, Ma Key—a Karen girl who kept house for Miss Gibbs—Mrs. Hare, and I, we prayed that God would mightily bless our feeble efforts, and as we prayed, the good news began to spread far and wide.

"Did y' hear? Did y' hear? Did y' hear?" called old Naw Kya Tee excitedly as she gathered some old ladies around her in a village eight miles away. "The God worshipers have built a 'disease house' down on the riverbank at Ohn Daw."

"At Ohn Daw!" chorused the old ladies incredulously. "Where the haunted pagoda is?"

"At Ohn Daw, the Village of Palm Trees," she assured them. "At Ohn Daw, where the haunted pagoda is, and they say the curse has no power over the God worshipers, and they say their medicine is powerful and they say ——"

"Of course their medicine is powerful," broke in one. "They are *dawtakas*. They are *dawtakas*. That's why their medicine is strong."

"Ha, ha, ha," laughed the crowd in approval.

"And if you just eat their medicine once, you come under their power," she went on.

"How do you know?" challenged Naw Kya Tee. "Have you ever as much as seen the white God worshipers? Have you ever as much as tasted ——"

"Me? No! No! I'll say not. Do I want to become the *dawtakas'* food?" replied the second speaker.

"Ha, ha, ha," laughed the crowd.

37

"Well, I'm going down to see the God worshipers and their disease house. I am. I am," continued Naw Kya Tee.

"You are?" chorused the crowd. "You'd better be careful, you'd better be careful. You know the devils don't like us to have anything to do with the God worshipers."

"I don't care what you say," defied Naw Kya Tee. "I *am* going down to see them. I've worshiped the devils all my life, and you know it, and they are no good, and you know that too. Have you forgotten last year how our buffaloes got sick, and we sacrificed our pigs and our chickens to the devils so that they could get better, but they didn't. They kept on dying just the same, and we kept on sacrificing our pigs and chickens till all our buffaloes were dead with disease and all our pigs and chickens were dead with sacrificing. Of course the devils are no good, and I don't care what you say, I *am* going down to see the white God worshipers for myself."

The crowd was silent with astonishment. Only too well they knew that she spoke the truth about the devils, but at last they began to shake their heads. "You'd better be careful. You'd better be careful," they said. "You know we are the slaves of the evil spirits, and we can't help it, but if you go down there, the devils will get angry, and then if any trouble comes to the village, it will all be your fault. It will all be your fault. And if it does we won't let you live here. We won't."

"I don't care what you do. I am going," insisted Naw Kya Tee, and the next day, calling her big eighteen-year-old daughter Hla Kin to accompany her, down to the dispensary she came. Naw Kya Tee was somewhat of a village doctor herself. She had traveled far more than the others in her village. She had been to Papun, sixty miles away,

38

where she bought dried rhinoceros blood, which she re-
tailed to pale, sick people for its weight in silver. She was
skilled in the use of charms and magic, and it was during
her travels that she heard of our dispensary and decided
to visit it.

"Anyway," she argued to herself, "haven't our fathers
always told us about God. Haven't we heard them sing—

> 'This earth in the beginning God made it,
> He can make it narrow, He can make it wide.
> This earth in the beginning God made it,
> He made it with its food and its drink.'

Haven't they told us that our white brother would come
on a white elephant, bringing back our golden book! Who
can tell but this might be our white brother! Who can tell
but they might have the golden book of God!"

So it was not long till she had crossed the river with her
big daughter and drew near the "white God worshipers'
disease house." Even as they neared it, however, a feeling of
fear overcame them. After all, her people might be right.
Maybe the God worshipers were *dawtakas*. They hid in
some bushes across the road for a while, so they could see
without being seen. And as they stood there, a mother with
a crying babe, and a man in agony, holding a painful ab-
scessed hand, went right inside. They didn't seem afraid,
and soon the mother came out with a happy, smiling babe
in her arms, and the man came out with a clean bandage
on his arm, his face wreathed in happiness.

"Look! Look! They didn't eat them! They didn't eat
them!" she gasped. "What are we frightened of? Come on,
we will go," and, joining another group that was just going
into the dispensary, they silently went up the steps and

stood wondering at all they saw. There was the white woman, Nurse Gibbs—so white. She was washing a man's sore hand—so gently. Then she put the ointment on and a clean bandage around it, and said, with a smile, "Come again, Uncle. Come tomorrow, and I'll put some more medicine on it."

Naw Kya Tee gasped. "The white woman speaks our words! She speaks our words!"

Accustomed to such exclamations, Nurse Gibbs looked up and smiled. "Of course we do, Aunty, and if we only had time we would come to visit with you in your homes. But there are so many sick people, and so many sick babies coming all day long that I never get a chance to go visiting. Do you know what I need, Aunty?" she went on as she turned to another patient. "I need a big girl to come and live with me. I need a girl about eighteen years old to help me wash the bandages and give the babies their castor oil and eye drops."

Naw Kya Tee's heart began to pound. She looked at her big girl Hla Kin. Nurse Gibbs hadn't even noticed her yet, but nothing escaped Hla Kin's eyes or ears. With her mouth wide open she waited for the next words. "Do you happen to know a big girl who would like to come to live with me, Aunty?"

For just a short second they both stood speechless, then grabbing her daughter, Naw Kya Tee pulled her forward, saying, "How would this one do?"

Miss Gibbs was thrilled. "Would you—would she—like to come?" she asked, almost afraid to hope.

"Of course she would like to come, and she can do many things to help the white Ma Ma."

Nurse Gibbs could hardly believe it. She stood up and

examined Hla Kin carefully. She was just the kind of girl she needed. She was just the kind of girl she had been praying for, so Hla Kin came to live at the mission station, and away back in the village where Naw Kya Tee lived, the old ladies whispered to each other, "Did y' hear? Did y' hear? That woman has let her daughter go to live with the God worshipers. Now you see, it won't be long before they eat her all up. It won't! It won't!"

But the God worshipers didn't eat her all up. They taught her how to work, and with her fearless help and continued presence the dispensary work increased and prospered.

Several months went happily by, then one morning we were surprised by an early visit from Hla Kin's married sister. "Thara! Thara! Come and see my poor sick mother quick. Mother thinks it's only fever, but the old ladies say it's the devils getting angry because Hla Kin is living here."

"Of course I'll come," I replied. Hadn't we come to dig for treasure? and didn't we expect it would be hard work to snatch the gold from the hands of the evil one?

"I'll be back by five o'clock," I called to Mrs. Hare as I left the house after a hasty breakfast. "And, if I'm not back by five o'clock, you will know that I've been invited to stay the night and have found an opportunity to preach."

I jumped into the mission launch with my medicine bag and went up the river a mile or two to the place where the trail to Kawmaley began.

"Come back for me about four o'clock," I called cheerfully to the launch driver, "but don't wait after five o'clock. I may stay in the village all night."

In the best of spirits I followed along with the little group that had called me, past a banana garden, through the

41

dense bamboo jungle, broken here and there by small clearings for rice cultivation, past "tiger village," where we had
held our first Sabbath school (of course, that wasn't its real
name, but the name I gave it because of the tiger skins we
found drying there), then away off toward the hills and
across the extensive rice fields to Kawmalay, a beautiful
village with its temples, coconut palms, and mango trees.

"I'm—so glad—you've come," whispered the sick
woman. "I think it's only fever, but the old ladies say it's
the devils, and I want them to see that the medicine of the
God worshipers is powerful."

I took her temperature, gave her some medicine, assured
her that it was not the devils and that she would soon be
better, then walked around the village a little. Nearly everybody was out at work and, though I treated several other
sick people, I felt that this was not the best time to try to
have an evening meeting. I was getting hungry too, and
the jungle folk would not eat till about four o'clock. I could
be home by then, for it was only eight miles. Knowing the
motor launch would be waiting for me, about two o'clock
I asked for someone to guide me back to the river. After a
little delay a little old man came with his bag on his shoulder
and his trusty knife at his side.

"I'll take you back to the river, Thara," he said, and
after one more look at my patient to make sure everything
was all right, we started off. The morning had been bright
and sunshiny, but I noticed that now the sky was overcast
with heavy black clouds. My guide noticed it too and quick-
ened his pace a little, but before we had crossed the first
expanse of rice fields, it began to rain, and soon we were
sopping wet. Hunger added to my discomfort. I looked at
my watch. It was already three-thirty.

"We must be near Tiger Village," I comforted myself, "and then it's only two miles to the launch and home and a good hot dinner."

But it was another half hour before we came to Tiger Village, and, when we did, the headman's house didn't seem to be in the right place. In some way we had come to it from the side, for there were hundreds of trails in the jungle.

"Come eat rice, Thara. Come eat rice!" they called as we passed through, but as home was only two miles away and we were wet and the launch would not wait after five, we thanked them and passed on. We were now in dense bamboo jungle, and it began to get dark. The rain came down heavier and heavier. The water dripped off my chin and soaked my topee and ran into my boots. I was beginning to feel miserable by the time we reached the first rice clearing.

"We are nearly there," I said to my guide. "There are only three of these clearings and then the river and the launch, and you must come home with me tonight."

He smiled. It would be an experience to eat white man's rice, and still smiling he plunged into the next bamboo thicket. I followed grimly. It still rained and thundered, but soon we came to the second clearing, and finally the third.

"We are there!" I shouted to my guide. "The river is next."

We picked up the trail out of the third rice cultivation. We were in water and mud over my boots, but what did that matter. The launch would be there. The bamboos began to thin out in front of us.

"Here we are," I shouted, and then with my hand on

43

my guide's arm stood stock still, because it was not the river but another cultivation carved out of the dense jungle.

"It must have been four fields to the river," he cried, and I followed on almost reluctantly as he picked up a trail and plunged forward into more dense jungle. But instead of leading to the river, it led to another cultivation.

"I'm sure there weren't five fields," I said. "The river must be somewhere here," was his answer as he tried unsuccessfully to break through the jungle to his right. We went around and around the field, but the only trail out was straight ahead.

"It must have been five fields," he remarked somewhat doubtfully, and again we went forward. I looked at my watch. It was after five o'clock. The launch surely had gone back. It was getting darker and darker, and it was still raining. I began to feel that maybe we were getting lost. The two big tiger skins in Tiger Village kept coming unpleasantly to my memory. "We must soon be there," I thought, but no, we were coming to another field.

"How long since you came this way?" I demanded of my now fearful guide.

"It must be twenty years since I came this way," he replied, "but then I knew every inch."

"Don't you know where we are now?" I asked frantically, but why I asked I don't know, for all of a sudden I realized that we were lost. If only we could find a hut—but there were no huts. If only we had some matches—but we had no matches. We stood around helplessly waiting for something to happen, but nothing happened. It only rained and rained and grew darker. It was six-thirty, and we were wet and tired and hungry and lost.

"I wish we ——," began my guide.

"We have no time to wish now," I interjected. "Follow me! We'll try to get back to Tiger Village where we can be safe for the night."

"But it's dark, Thara."

"Never mind; we can't stay here. We have to do something. Come on," I commanded, and turning, we plunged into the gloom of the thick bamboo jungle. We could move only one step at a time. With our hands in front, we groped along. It seemed hours before we came to the next clearing, but after getting on our knees and feeling with our hands, we picked up the outward trail.

"Oh, God, send an angel to guide us back," I prayed, and I seemed to see a shadowy form beckoning us on, but of a sudden my palpitating heart froze in fear, for the shadow resembled more the shape of a lurking tiger. The next minute, however, I relaxed and went limp all over as we passed an old tree stump. Thus we crawled back, on and on, inch by inch. Soon all the courage of my guide gave way. "We're lost! We're lost! We're lost!" he moaned. "The spirits are against us! The spirits are against us! I fear they'll ——" Suddenly he broke off, listened a moment, and clutched my arm. "Listen! Listen!" he shrieked. "Listen!"

I stood still a moment and listened. Not far away above the pounding of the heavy rain could be heard a distinct grumbling roar. All I could think of was tigers! All my guide could think of was spirits, but as we tuned our ears to this new noise, gradually we realized that it was a little creek we had passed earlier in the afternoon. Yet, though recollecting it was only a creek, we wondered whether we could cross it in the darkness, for the only bridge, a pole about six inches through and about fifteen feet long, might

45

not still be there. It could easily have been washed away in the rising waters. It could ——

"Oh, Thara," broke in my guide. "It's no use! It's no use! We're lost! We can't get across that stream. I feel the evil spirits around me. I feel—I feel—Thara, I feel that—a curse—some terrible curse has caught up with us."

3

Finding Valuable Ore

><><><><><><><><><

"*Again, the kingdom of heaven is like unto treasure hid in a field; the which when a man hath found, he hideth, and for joy thereof goeth and selleth all that he hath, and buyeth that field.*" Matthew 13:44.

"Thara Is Every Bit as Good Looking as Adam and Eve Were in the Garden of Eden"

3

Finding Valuable Ore

✕✕✕✕✕✕✕✕✕✕

CAUTIOUSLY WE CREPT FORWARD. Shrouded in the darkness somewhere in front of us was the swollen creek. When our ears told us that we were right upon it, we got on our knees and crawled, feeling for the six-inch log bridge. .

"It's here! It's here! It's still here!" I shouted to my companion as I found the log still a little above the swift water. "Here, you hold this end till I get across; then I'll hold the other end while you get across."

Then carefully straddling the pole, with my feet dangling in the water, I pulled myself across little by little. In a minute or two my companion came across, and on we went in the darkness and the rain.

Creeping, crawling, stumbling for seemingly endless hours, we journeyed and then, "A light! A light! Look, we're there! It's Tiger Village!" I cried and made straight for the light.

In my delight I hadn't figured that, of course, the trail to the light would not be straight, so the next thing I knew

I had stumbled right over a low barricade into horrible smelly mud. It turned out to be a pigsty, and the pigs strongly objected to late-comers. They raced round and round, grunting and snorting, and no one could ever have told who of us was the most terrified. I only know that by the time I got out of that pigsty I must have been a shocking sight. It was no wonder that, when I knocked on the bamboo wall of the house where the light was, the woman screamed, "Who are you? Who are you?"

"It's me, Aunty," I called, "the white Thara of Ohn Daw."

"Oh, no, it's not! No, it's not!" she yelled. "He's been drowned, and this is his ghost come to haunt me."

"I'm no ghost, Aunty," I said. "I've been lost, and I can't find my way home. Please show me where the headman's house is."

"Well," she said, calming down, "if it's really you yourself, that's the headman's house over there by that coconut palm," and in a few minutes we were with friends. I was surprised to find it was just eight-thirty.

"We are so glad you found your way back, Thara," said the headman kindly. "You may never have lived through the night in a storm like that."

His good wife quickly brought us a plate of hot rice each and a little square of dried fish. Oh, but it did taste good, and I was hungry enough to do it justice. While I feasted, my good hostess stood eying my bedraggled appearance, and as I washed my hands, she said, "Now, Thara, you'll have to change your clothes. You can't sleep in those dirty, muddy things."

"But, Aunty," I said, "this is all I have."

"Oh, that doesn't matter," she said, throwing a little

bundle to me. "Here is a loincloth. Put that on while I rinse out your things."

After pondering the situation for a second, I decided to make the best of it and, going inside I took off my dirty wet clothes and came forth adorned in the loincloth. Now, it was perfectly modest and covered me from my hips to my knees, but, of course, there was quite a lot of Brother Hare on the outside and, while my clothes were being rinsed, I went over to the fireplace to keep warm. Soon my hostess was sitting on the other side of the fireplace drying my clothes, and the world began to take on a happier and more comfortable aspect. In a minute or two, however, we had visitors. Three neighborly grandmothers, feeling that something interesting was going on at the headman's house, had come to see, and now sat with my hostess on the other side of the open fireplace. Taking advantage of the opportunity, they at once joined my anatomy class, and after studying me in silence, presently began to recite aloud. Said the first one, "Look at his white chest! If his face was white like that, wouldn't he be pretty?"

Said the second, "Look at his arms! The top half is white like a white man, and the bottom half is brown like a Karen."

Said number three, "And look! Even his long legs are white! Whoever would have thought that his legs would be white!"

Then my hostess—bless her heart—came to my rescue. "Never mind, you ladies," she said. "Thara is every bit as good looking as Adam and Eve were in the Garden of Eden."

I smiled too when I told Mrs. Hare the next day, but it wasn't a bit funny that stormy night. I was grateful to be safe, and doubly grateful to realize that the jungle folk were remembering the Bible stories I had been telling them. Even the hard bamboo floor felt soft and friendly as, dressed once more in my own dry clothes, I lay down to sleep. In the morning it was very easy to find our way to the river. We discovered that there were two trails out of the third rice clearing. One led into the trouble of the day before; the other led straight to the river.

.   .   .   .   .

I cannot say too much in praise of the efficient, faithful work done by Nurse Mary Gibbs during those months in the little jungle dispensary. Had not the old village headman said, "Nobody will come, for fear of the haunted pagoda?"

He didn't know. He forgot to realize that the devil worshipers feared nothing more than death, and in spite of his fears and his prophecies they came. Sick babies, sick mothers, sick uncles, sick aunties—nearly dead with malaria, dysentery, and pneumonia; almost frantic with the pain from sore eyes, aching teeth, terrible boils, and abscesses; loathsome with skin diseases and ringworm— Miss Gibbs cared for them all. Wherever I went as I attempted to visit these patients in their villages, I carried a medicine bag, and we were thus able to save hundreds of lives and make hundreds of friends. The need and the sorrow spurred us ever on and drove us nearer and nearer to the side of the loving Physician who had promised to be with us always.

"Doctor, doctor," cried a man in a village twelve miles away from our dispensary, "have you got any burn medicine?"

"Surely I have," I replied. "When did your little girl burn herself?"

"When? Oh, about seven years ago," was his surprising reply.

"But what can I do for a burn seven years old?" I groaned.

"Well, come up and have a look anyway," he urged.

So I climbed up the little bamboo ladder into his house. In the dim light I could see nothing, for there were no windows to their huts. I heard him call his daughter to come. In answer I heard something that sounded like a kangaroo hopping. The next minute a twelve-year-old girl stood before me on one leg while her father told me, "When she was a little tot five years old, one evening her dress caught on fire, and it burned all of one leg, one side of her body, and one arm. Then, because we had no medicine, and because the missionaries hadn't come yet, and because the government hospital was too far away, and because it hurt to be exposed to the air, she huddled in the corner in the darkness and cried. In six months her little leg and body had grown together." He looked hopefully into my face for a moment, then pleaded, "Now, doctor, have you some burn medicine to give her so that she can run and walk and play like other children again?"

"Oh, you must take her to the hospital in Moulmein," I cried. "No! No! We are afraid of the hospital in Moulmein. It's too far away. Please won't you give her some medicine so that she can run and walk and play again?"

Of course I had no medicine like that, and pausing only to tell her of a God who had power to save and make whole all who believe on Him, I hurried on with a heavy heart.

"Doctor, doctor," cried a jungle mother near by with a

two-year-old baby on her arm. "Doctor, I think my baby has
the toothache."

I said, "It surely has something of the kind," for it was
screaming at the top of its voice and scratching and clawing
at its little mouth. On opening its mouth, I found that it had
had a tooth infection and the tooth had rotted out. I cleaned
up the place where the tooth had been, but as there seemed
to be a little piece of the root left, I selected a sharp-pointed
pair of forceps and tried to pull it out, but I pulled out
instead three wriggling maggots!

Can you wonder I talk of need? Can you wonder that
I say it spurred us on? Our medical work was not without
its results. Only in the new villages did we hear the cry
of "*Dawtaka, Dawtaka*" any more, and wherever we had
been the people began to call us the "white brother" and to
ask, "When are you going to start a school at Ohn Daw?
We want our children whose lives you have saved to go to
your school and learn about God."

At the dispensary they talked in the same way to Nurse
Gibbs. We began to make a list, and soon we had the names
of fifty boys and girls who wanted to come to the mission
school. I took the list to our mission committee in Rangoon
and begged for a teacher. They rejoiced with me over the
prospects and called a faithful young Karen man from our
training school at Meiktila, whose name was Peter, to be the
teacher of the Ohn Daw school.

On our way up the river we laid our plans, and though
we had only one small bamboo house available we decided
to advertise our school at once and get started as soon as
possible. Accordingly the next week we went everywhere,
all around our district visiting our old dispensary friends and
broadcasting everywhere, "Next Monday at nine o'clock in

the morning we are going to open school. Be sure to come next Monday morning."

"Ugh! Ugh! Ah! Ah!" grunted our friends as they smiled at the news.

So it was with light hearts that we opened school at nine o'clock next Monday morning—that is, we opened the school *house*. We opened up the front door, dusted off the seats, put a piece of chalk in front of the blackboard, and put the chair behind the table, and then I walked up and down with my watch in my hand, waiting for the boys and girls to come. And I walked up and down, and walked up and down, but nobody came, and I said to Peter, "Now what are we going to do?"

"Well," he said thoughtfully, "you know the jungle folks don't know the days of the week very well. Maybe they have got mixed up, and they think it's tomorrow!"

"Oh, then," I said, "we'll open school again tomorrow." And so we did—that is, we opened the school *house*. We opened up the front door and dusted off the seats and put the piece of chalk in front of the blackboard and put the chair behind the table. Then again I walked up and down with my watch in my hand waiting for the boys and girls to come. I walked up and down and walked up and down, but it was no use. Nobody came! So I said to Peter, "Now what are we going to do?"

And he said, "Maybe, Thara, they expect us to go and bring the children to school!"

And I said, "Maybe they do. Then tomorrow morning instead of opening school we will go over to Kawmaley and get Ton Pey and Naw Too, Hla Kin's little brother and sister. I just know they are going to come."

So the next morning, instead of opening school, we

55

crossed the river and away we went to Kawmaley, eight miles away. When we got there, sure enough, Ton Pey and Naw Too were all ready. Their mats were all rolled up and their slates and clothes all tied in a big handkerchief. Smiling as they saw us, they said, "We just knew you would come. That's why we didn't go yesterday or the day before."

"All right, here we are. Let's go!" I urged, "because no one has come yet, and I suppose everybody else is waiting for someone to come first," and taking Naw Too with one hand and Ton Pey with the other, we were just about to start off when Naw Kya Tee said, "Oh, Thara, Ton Pey has been going down to the Buddhist school. I think he had better go and get his certificate of transfer. He will only be a minute."

So we sat down for a minute while Ton Pey got over the fence and went down the trail toward the temple school after his certificate of transfer. We waited ten minutes, and Ton Pey didn't come back.

"Whatever do you suppose is keeping him?" I asked the mother.

"I don't know, Thara," she said, "but don't worry. I'll just run down and have a look." And she got over the fence and disappeared down the trail that led to the temple school.

We waited ten more minutes, but she didn't come back.

"Do you suppose something has happened to Ton Pey?" I asked the married sister.

"I don't know, I'm sure," she said, "but don't worry, Thara, I'll go and have a look." And she got over the fence and disappeared down the trail that led to the temple school.

We waited ten more minutes, but she didn't come back. Then the aunty went to have a look, and she didn't come

56

back. Last of all, the grandma went to have a look, and she didn't come back.

"Peter," I said, after waiting ten more minutes, "whatever can have happened?"

"I don't know, I'm sure, Thara," he said, "but don't you worry, I'll ——"

"No, you won't," I said. "If anybody else has to go, I'll go myself." Getting over the fence, I started off down the trail that led to the temple school to have a look, and what do you think I saw? The yellow-robed, shaven-headed Buddhist priest was standing on the steps of his schoolhouse, cursing the white God worshipers. "Of course I won't let one of my boys sit at the feet of a Christian dog!" he growled, and the mother, the sister, the aunty, and the grandma knelt in the dust, afraid to move. He was speaking in Burmese, however, and I couldn't understand what he said.

"Where's Ton Pey?" I asked in Karen, and half a dozen boys pointed to Ton Pey, crying behind the door. Then I did something terrible. I wouldn't do it now, but I didn't know any better then. Do you know what I did? I walked right up the steps into the Buddhist school with my boots on. *With my boots on!* It was too terrible for words. The priest was speechless.

"Come on, Ton Pey," I said, taking his hand and going out. "Come on, mother, sister, aunty, grandma. We don't need any certificate of transfer." They got up and followed me back to the house.

As we moved away, the priest's tongue was loosed, and you should have heard the abuse. "I wish," he yelled, "that in the next life the Christian dog is born into a cow with horns on and after that into a slimy maggot."

57

But by the time this was translated to me we had reached the house, and it didn't matter. We just took a deep breath, heaved a big sigh, and saying good-by, went off with Ton Pey and Naw Too to Ohn Daw. The next day we began school. We opened up the front door, dusted off the chairs, and put the piece of chalk in front of the blackboard. Peter sat on the chair behind the table, while Ton Pey sat at one end and Naw Too at the other.

"Be faithful, Peter," I called, "while I go out and bring back some more."

Then off I went to some more villages. At night I came back and inquired, "Did any more children come today, Peter?"

"No, Thara; how many did you get?" he replied.

"Oh, they are coming tomorrow, Peter," I said, and the next day Peter taught school with two children while I went to gather some more. But they didn't come that day or the next day or the next. For three weeks Peter taught school with Ton Pey and Naw Too while I canvassed and canvassed the country for more children, but none came.

Naw Doo was all ready to come, but her father had had a bad dream, so she couldn't leave. Aung Too was just leaving the house when his little sister cut her finger, and that was a bad sign, so he couldn't come. The baby cried when Tun Maung was getting ready, and a plate broke when Saw Thoo was eating his breakfast, so of course they couldn't come. But behind all these bad omens and signs was the all-absorbing fear that maybe, after all, the white God worshipers were *dawtakas* and would feed their children and fatten them up and then eat them. Anyway, the yellow-robed priests said they would, and so the children were not permitted to come.

58

After we had tried unsuccessfully for three weeks to get them to school, Peter said, "Thara, what are we going to do now?"

"Peter," I said, "there's only *one* more thing we *can* do. Come and I will show you." And we got on our knees around the dear old Book and opened the pages to Isaiah 55:8-11. Then we prayed, "Lord, Thou hast said Thy word shall not return unto Thee void, but it shall accomplish that which Thou desirest, and it shall prosper in the thing whereto thou hast sent it." Then we told the Lord that we had done all we could and had no strength to do more, but since He had the power and there was nothing impossible for Him, we believed He would help us find the treasure hidden beneath all this fear and superstition.

And do you know, right away something began to happen. The very next day two more children came from Mezita. Then one from No Ta, two more from Thadaoo, and one from Kawlone, and by the end of the next week we had ten students.

You can have no idea of how many ten can be till you have worked for them as hard as we worked for that ten. How they rejoiced my heart! I counted them in the morning when we got up, I counted them when they went to school, I counted them at play, and I counted them when they went to bed at night. One, two, three, four, five, six, seven, eight, nine, ten. Our school was established at last, and I knew that, given a chance, it would grow.

We taught them how to sing "Jesus Loves Me! This I Know," "Long Ago the Children Sang a Song," and "When He Cometh to Gather His Jewels." We taught them to sing soprano and alto. Peter sang bass and I sang tenor. Then we put them into our bullock wagon or our motor launch and took them to their villages, and, standing up in a little ring, we sang to their mothers and fathers and aunties and uncles. They crowded around. "Who are these that sing?" they said. "Are these angels from heaven?"

"Why, no," I replied. "They are your own children. Look, don't you know them?"

"Oh, no, they are not! Our children don't comb their hair like that. Our children don't have clean clothes like that. Our children don't have shiny faces like that," they said, shaking their heads.

"But they are your children," I persisted. "Look, here's Naw Doo."

And Naw Doo's mother looked at her own little girl for the longest time till finally a smile broke on her face and she said, "Why so it is! So it is! The *dawtakas* haven't eaten her after all."

And from that moment we knew that we were getting nearer and nearer the treasure in the land of the haunted pagoda. With hardly an effort our attendance increased to twenty-six the next year, and the year after that it increased to thirty-four, and our joy would have been complete but for the fact that furlough time had arrived for our faithful Nurse Gibbs and we had to say good-by to her for a time. However, that year, as if to make up for the loneliness and added burdens, God gave us the first fruits of our labors.

I will never forget the day when Hla Kin said to me, "Thara, I've been here nearly three years now, and I've learned to work, and I've learned to read. Every spare moment I've had I have been reading the Golden Book, and I've found Jesus, and I believe He is the Son of God, and, Thara, I would like to be baptized and become a God worshiper too."

"Bless your heart, Hla Kin," I said. "Next time mother comes down we will ask her what she thinks of it, and then we will make arrangements for you to be baptized."

In a few days, when Naw Kya Tee happened to be coming by, I said, "Aunty, your big girl wants to be baptized and become a God worshiper. How do you feel about it?"

"I don't care if she does," she replied. "We have worshiped the devils all our lives, and they are no good. I don't care if she does become a God worshiper. Maybe when I know a little more I might become a God worshiper too."

So we called for an ordained minister to come and baptize Hla Kin, for I was not ordained at the time, and who do you think came? Pastor A. H. Williams, who, with Pastor J. A. Hamilton, had discovered Ohn Daw as a mission site.

What a happy day it was for us. Our boys and girls and a few friends stood around on the riverbank singing "Happy Day, Happy Day, When Jesus Washed My Sins Away," while Hla Kin was baptized in the great Salween River. We had found treasure at last, treasure more valuable than gold.

But away back in the village where Hla Kin's mother lived, it was a different story. "Did y' hear? Did y' hear?" called the old ladies in excitement. "Those God worshipers took that woman's daughter and dipped her right down underneath the water! Oh, isn't it terrible! Isn't it terrible! Now they will come to our village and catch all of us and dip us all down under the water. Oh, what will we do? What will we do? We won't let her live here anymore, we won't. We won't have her here any longer, we won't."

So they called the Buddhist priest, and had him curse poor old Naw Kya Tee and her house and her children. Then with sticks and stones they drove her away.

"What will I do now, Thara?" she appealed to me the next day. "They have driven me out."

"Well, Aunty," I replied, "I think their anger will soon pass over when they see that nothing happens, and I can get police protection for you if you wish, you know, for the British Government guarantees religious freedom to each of its subjects."

"No, no, Thara. I don't want to live there anymore. I want to go away."

"Then," I said, "Hla Kin and your two little children are here. You just go off visiting some of your relatives and think things over for a week or two."

So everything worked out all right for Naw Kya Tee, but back in her village there was more trouble. They say that after she left, because there was no one to put the rice on the spirit altar each day, the devils got angry and came down and haunted that house, and at night the village folk were terrified with the screaming and yelling and groaning that issued forth from the empty house.

"We can't stand it," said the elders as they gathered in the village council. "The house is worse than the old woman. It is! It is!"

"What shall we do?" asked the headman.

"I know, I know," said one. "Let us burn it down."

"Fine! Fine!" chorused the elders.

"You strike the first match," ordered the headman.

"Oh, no, not me. I'm afraid of the devils. Not me, not me," they cried, and not a man there was brave enough to strike the first match to burn it down.

"I know," cried another. "Let us pull it down! We can all pull a board off and ——"

"Fine! Fine!" chorused the elders.

"You pull the *first* board off," ordered the headman of the one who had suggested the plan.

"Oh, no! no! I couldn't do that. I'm afraid!" he cried, and not a man in the crowd was found brave enough to pull the first board off.

"I know," said another. "Let's send for the old woman and make her come and pull it down herself."

"Fine! Fine!" chorused the elders.

"You go and call the old woman," ordered the headman.

So off he went across the rice fields, through the jungle, to Kawlone, where poor old Naw Kya Tee was taking refuge, and the next day she stood before me again, telling me of her trouble.

"I'm only a little old woman," she cried. "How can I pull a house down? How I wish I could sell it somehow. I would like to go and live somewhere else."

Now it just happened—or did it *just* happen?—that five days before, I had received two hundred rupees from the mission committee to build a new house for our boys. Our school was growing, and I was looking around for some lumber to build with, so I said, "Aunty, are the posts of your house still good?"

"Good as the day the house was built," she replied. "We got the best hardwood posts."

"And are the floor boards still good?" I inquired further.

"Just as good as can be."

"Then why don't you sell the house to me if you really don't want to live in it," I said, "and I'll go over and pull the house down."

"Oh, Thara, if you would I'd sell it to you for fifty rupees," she said.

The next day we went to see the village elders, and I

63

proposed that they let me pay her fifty rupees for the posts
and the floor boards, then I'd come with some of my big
boys and pull the old house down. They were delighted.
They didn't care what the devils did to the white God worshipers, the more the better, the quicker the sooner, so they
encouraged me to come as soon as possible and take the
old haunted house away.

In a few days, with half a dozen bullock wagons and
about a dozen big boys and some crowbars and hammers, we
arrived all ready for business.

"Here they are! Here they are!" excitedly called the
villagers to each other. "Come and let us see what the devils
will do," and they stood around us in a big circle expecting
to see the devils utterly demolish the God worshipers, but
what do you think they saw? They saw the big boys from
the mission school climbing up on the posts onto the roof
till at last they sat straddle-legged on the top of the
haunted house while they sang and whistled "Onward
Christian Soldiers, Marching As to War." That's what they
saw! And one by one the pieces of leaf thatch were thrown
down. One by one the bamboo rafters were thrown down.
One by one the floor boards were pulled up, and one by one
the posts were pulled over till by noon the whole house was
torn down, and nobody's head had been crushed, nobody's
arms or legs had been broken, and as far as we knew,
nobody had even gotten a splinter in his finger.

The devil worshipers couldn't believe it. Their devils
had no power over the God worshipers! Taking one more
look to make sure it was true, they turned and ran to their
houses and huts to hide themselves. We soon had our
wagons loaded, and by evening the old haunted house was
carted to the riverbank opposite our mission station.

"Well, Peter," I said, surveying the pile of lumber and posts, "How are we going to get this across the river? We can't load it into the launch or canoe. They are not big enough. What have you got to suggest?"

"I've been thinking, Thara," he replied. "Some of these posts are too heavy to float but some of them are light and I believe that, if we tie them all together in a raft, it will float enough so that we can pull it across the river with the launch.'

"Splendid, Peter!" I exclaimed, and the next day we put some skids in the shallow water, drove in some posts at the end, and began to make our raft. When it was done we tied big ropes around it, pulled out the posts, and levered it off into the deep water, and it floated! It did! It did! About half an inch above the water. We brought the launch, tied a big rope securely to the back of the launch, then headed upstream so that when the current caught us and swung us downstream we would land somewhere on our mission property. The engine chugged away courageously. We gained momentum with our raft, and I was rejoicing at our success when all of a sudden Peter grabbed my arm and, pointing out of the back of the launch, shouted out, "Look, Thara, look!"

I looked, but everything seemed all right. There was a little ripple behind the launch flowing gently over the raft, but our ropes were holding, and all seemed well. "What's the matter, Peter? It's all right," I assured him.

"But, Thara, look! Look!" he still shouted.

"Yes, but look what?" I asked quite puzzled.

"Why, look, Thara! The water is going right over the house. The house is getting baptized! The house is getting baptized!"

5   65

"Sure enough, so it is," I said. "Peter, this is our second convert."

And do you know that house *was* converted. In just three weeks it was rebuilt on the mission property. The same old posts, the same old boards, new bamboo walls, and a new leaf roof. There was only one part of the old house that we didn't use, and that was the spirit altar built onto the middle post upstairs. We threw it into the river to be carried away to the depths of the ocean, and just where the altar used to be, Peter put his study table. Right where the offering plate used to be, Peter kept his Bible. Instead of the screaming and yelling of evil spirits every evening, the boys gathered around and sang, "What a wonderful change in my life has been wrought, since Jesus came into my heart." How we rejoiced to see the powers of darkness beginning to fall back!

The story of the house was told everywhere. Hundreds of people began to lose faith in the devils, and the next year fifty-seven students enrolled in our school. Another teacher was added to our staff, and prospects were never better when one day Peter came to me quite worried.

"Thara," he said, "we will have to do something about our drinking water. The river is too dirty and too full of germs to drink without boiling it, and by the time we let it settle, then boil it, the children are so thirsty that they drink it all while it is hot, so that we have to boil another canful."

"I know, Peter," I sympathized, "I've been thinking about it for a long time, and I think we had better dig a well."

"Splendid!" he said. "I'm so glad you know how to dig a well."

"But I don't," I replied. "I've never even helped to dig a well in all my life."

"Then what will we do, for I don't know how," responded Peter sadly.

"Don't let that worry you for a minute," I encouraged. "We'll dig a well anyway."

And so we did. That is, we dug a hole, and though it was six feet across at the top and only three feet across at the bottom, at a depth of forty feet we struck water—beautiful, clear, sparkling, fresh water. Unless you have dug a well you can't imagine how good it feels to strike water. I was on the shift at work when a shovelful of gravel was dug out and a shovelful of water took its place. What shouting and yelling and rejoicing there was. The buckets raced up and down at double speed till we had two feet of lovely, clear water in our well. Then I crawled up, went home, had a bath, changed my clothes, and walked up and down on the veranda, feeling good all over. I was still walking up and down on the veranda, feeling good all over, when Peter came rushing up the stairs.

"Thara, we're in trouble again!" he cried.

"What is it this time?" I groaned.

"Our well is caving in, Thara! The gravel is so soft that, as we draw the water out we can hear it caving in."

"Don't worry another minute, Peter," said I. "All we have to do is to brick our well up. You know, everybody bricks up wells so they can't cave in."

"Yes, but, Thara, where are we going to get the bricks?"

"There are all the bricks you need in the world at Moulmein, Peter."

"Yes, Thara, but it takes five days to get there, five to get back, and in ten days our well will all be spoiled."

"Well, can't we get some bricks near by somewhere?"

"I've already inquired, Thara, and there isn't a brick within twenty miles of us for sale."

"Then we'll have to sit down and think, Peter."

"Well, sit down quick, Thara, and think quick. Our well is caving in."

So we sat down and thought and thought—and—"Peter," I said suddenly. "I know—what about the old haunted ———."

"Oh, yes," broke in Peter. "Why didn't I think about that before? The old haunted pagoda!"

Taking a dozen of our big boys and a dozen hoes, we went to the old pagoda, dug over the ruins, and what do you think we found? Four thousand good, whole bricks! We put them in rice sacks, carried them on our shoulders, and brought them to our well, which we lined with all those fine bricks from the old haunted pagoda.

"Peter," I said, as we laid the last of the bricks, layer by layer, about halfway up from the bottom of the well, "Peter, we have found the treasure, haven't we?"

"Surely we have, Thara—real treasure! And just to think, God had these bricks made for us and carted to the mission station for us before we were born!"

"Ah, yes, it's wonderf———" I began to reply, but just then a groan, a howl, clear and distinct, seeming to come from the very bricks we had just put down, startled us.

"Did you hear that, Peter?" I inquired, but he didn't answer, because the sound came again louder and more distinct than before. We looked at each other. We knew our faces had suddenly gone pale, and Peter's voice trembled as he said, "Do you think—it might be the curse? Has the curse overtaken us?"

68

Shining Diamonds

>‹>‹>‹>‹>‹>‹>‹>‹>‹

"It cannot be gotten for gold, neither shall
silver be weighed for the price thereof. It
cannot be valued with the gold of Ophir,
with the precious onyx, or the sapphire. The
gold and the crystal cannot equal it: and the
exchange of it shall not be for jewels of
fine gold." Job 28:15-17.

Ohn Bwint Had to Swim Across Twenty Rivers and Walk Through Six Miles of Mud and Water Up to His Armpits to Get His Reports In on Time

Shining Diamonds

>+>+>+>+>+>+>+>+>+

THE GROANING AND HOWLING increased till
it echoed and re-echoed all through the well. At first petri-
fied with fear, we were now suddenly spurred to frantic
action, and began to climb up for all we were worth. The
nearer to the top we came, however, the louder and louder
the howling became, till at last, as we poked our heads
out—there it was! For a moment I sat quite limp until
Peter took his place panting beside me. Greatly relieved,
we smiled as we turned to comfort the little seven-year-old
boy who stood there just breaking his heart.

"What's the matter, Aung Thein?" I asked, patting the
little fellow on the back. "What's the matter?"

"Ooooo—Boohoo-oooo," he wailed louder and louder as
the tears rolled down his face. "Loo-oook up the-eeere! The
monkey's got my boo-ooook! Oooooo!"

We looked, and there, sure enough, in the nearest
mango tree sat our pet monkey tearing Aung Thein's book
to pieces. Many and many a time no doubt he had looked at

71

the little folks enviously as they went past his house with their books to school. Many and many a time, no doubt, he had wished he had a book. If ever he got the chance, he would show them how to read, and this day when he had slipped unnoticed out of his house, what was his good fortune but to see little Aung Thein drop his book while curiously looking down the well. Quick as a flash he grabbed it. Up the tree out of reach he scampered. Then, holding onto a branch with his tail, he held the book with his two feet, while he turned and tore the pages as fast as he could with his two hands. It was really one of the funniest things I have ever seen, and we were so relieved to find the actual source of the terrible noise we had heard while laying the bricks in the well that I said, "Never mind, Aung Thein, you come with me, and I'll get you another new book," and in a few moments his little heart was comforted and all was well.

About this time I made a surprising discovery. As I was continuing my study of Karen I read a folklore story about Mr. Rabbit. It was one of those stories that the jungle folk tell around their campfires and hand down from generation to generation. It went something like this:

Years and years ago a baby elephant and a baby tiger were born in the same part of the forest, and became fast friends. They played together. They grew up together, and took an oath of eternal brotherhood. After they were fully grown, one day the tiger stretched and yawned, and said to the elephant, "I'm full grown now, so I must do as all full-grown tigers do. Tomorrow morning I'm going to eat you for breakfast."

"But," objected the elephant in surprise, "you can't eat me. Why, we're brothers."

72

"My father eats elephants; my grandfathers ate elephants; so I'm going to eat elephants," said the tiger.

"But our brotherhood oath is stronger than death! You can't eat me!" argued the elephant.

"Custom is stronger than all laws," growled the tiger.

"But I'm bigger than you!"

"I am the strongest!"

"But you promised ——"

"Custom is stronger ——"

They argued and quarreled till finally the tiger said, "I'll tell you what we'll do. We will go over to the little hut at the foot of the hill. Then you shall make the biggest noise you can, and after that I'll make the biggest noise I can, and then we will listen to what the men say."

So over to the little hut at the foot of the hill they went, and the elephant lifted up his trunk and trumpeted as loud as he could. He made such a noise that the trees shook.

When he finished, they listened and heard the men in the hut say, "Oh! listen to the baby elephant crying!" "I wonder what makes the little elephant cry!"

"Now it's my turn," said the tiger, and he opened his mouth and growled, and growled, and growled until not only the trees but also the ground shook.

Then they listened, and inside the hut the men said, "No wonder the baby elephant cries! The full-grown tiger is going to eat him all up!"

"There you are!" triumphed the tiger. "You see, they call you baby elephant, and they call me a full-grown tiger. So I am going to eat you all up."

"Mercy! Mercy!" pleaded the elephant, "remember our boyhood days."

"Well, then, I'll tell you what I will do," said the tiger.

"Just because of our friendship I will give you six weeks to reap your rice, repair your house, and say good-by to your family, but the next morning you must come to this very spot, and then I'll eat you."

Away went the elephant in sorrow and tears, and he cried, and he cried, and he cried. He reaped his rice, he repaired his house, he said good-by to his family, and he cried, and he cried, and he cried. He cried so hard, and tears flowed so fast that he became very thirsty, so he stood by the river and drank, and drank, and drank, and cried, and cried, and cried, and his tears flowed down his trunk into the river, and made it all salty.

Now just at this time Grandfather Rabbit came hopping along for a drink, but on tasting the water, he spat it out quickly and said furiously, "Who's making all my water salty? I'll just walk along and see about this."

So he started off up the bank of the river, hippity-hop, hippity-hop. Soon he came to Mr. Elephant, who was crying so hard that his tears flowed down his trunk into the river and made all the water salty.

"What do you mean," he yelled to the elephant, "by making my water all salty?"

"Oh, Mr. Rabbit," cried the elephant, "if you only knew the trouble I am in, you wouldn't be angry with me; you'd feel sorry for me and would try to help me."

"What trouble is so great that your tears make the whole river salty?" demanded Mr. Rabbit.

"My lifelong tiger friend is going to eat me tomorrow morning."

"But didn't you take the brotherhood oath?"

"Yes, we did, but now that he is full grown he claims custom is stronger than all laws and promises."

74

"Custom! Custom!" muttered Mr. Rabbit in disgust. "Why don't you hire me for your lawyer? I could win your case with that old rascal."

"Oh, Mr. Rabbit, if you *could,* and if you *will* save my life, I will work for you forever."

"I only require that you obey me, and do just exactly what I tell you."

"I will!" cried the elephant with joy. "Just tell me what to do."

"Then listen! We will practice. Now, lie down!" commanded the rabbit, "and look as though you were dead."

And the elephant lay down and looked as if he were dead.

"Now, when you feel me lifting on your foot or your ear, you lift them up so that it looks as if I am lifting them up." So the elephant lifted up a foot or an ear when the rabbit pulled on them, and made it look as if the rabbit were doing it all.

"Now, if you feel me pulling on your tail or your trunk, you turn round and round in the direction I pull, so it will look as if I am doing it all," commanded Mr. Rabbit. And the elephant twisted this way and that way, so that it looked as if the rabbit were doing it all.

"Fine!" smiled the rabbit, "Fine! I will meet you before daybreak at the spot the tiger has named."

The night passed slowly, and at the appointed time the elephant went to meet the rabbit.

"Here I am," whispered Mr. Rabbit as the elephant approached through the darkness. "Now remember! Make it look as though I am doing it with my great strength."

The elephant lay down. Mr. Rabbit jumped on top of him and began a wild dance. He danced on one leg, he

75

danced on two; then he sprang to the ground and lifted one huge elephant leg, then another, and then an ear. Then he twisted him around by the tail this way and by the trunk that way. Then he danced and he danced.

In the midst of this strange performance Mr. Tiger crept hungrily toward his breakfast, but as he came to the spot, what a sight met his eyes! Mr. Rabbit dancing on his elephant! lifting a leg! an ear! twisting that great big elephant around.

"Dear me," said the tiger to himself, "I've always heard of the marvelous strength and power of Grandfather Rabbit, but I never dreamed he could do anything like this! I had better speak to him very politely, for one can never tell what Mr. Rabbit will do next."

Then coming up a little closer, Mr. Tiger said politely, "Good morning, Mr. Rabbit. When you have finished playing with my elephant, just leave him there. I'm going to eat him for breakfast."

Mr. Rabbit stopped his dancing just long enough to say, "Who said it was your elephant, cheeky face? When did you kill this elephant indeed? Now look here, my striped friend, I'm just giving you a word of warning. I've had six elephants already for my breakfast this morning, and this is my seventh, and if you stay around here much longer, when I'm finished with him, I'll start on you."

"Dear me," said the tiger to himself. "I can't argue with Mr. Rabbit myself. I'd better get a lawyer to speak for me," and off he went through the forest looking for a lawyer. But when the animals heard they had to argue with Grandfather Rabbit, none of them dared to accept the case, till the tiger came to Mr. Monkey.

Now because Mr. Monkey had a secret ambition to ride

on the back of the king of the forest, he said, "Oh, yes, I'd just be glad to be your lawyer, Mr. Tiger. I can chatter better than any animal in the forest, but I have a sore foot and I couldn't walk so far."

"Never mind the foot," urged the tiger; "I'll let you ride on my back."

The monkey then jumped onto the back of Mr. Tiger, and they started off. But the skin of the tiger was too loose, and although he held on with his two hands and his two feet, the monkey flopped helplessly from side to side.

"Wait! Wait!" called the monkey breathlessly. "You must tie me on. Your skin is too loose." So the tiger got some long jungle creepers and tied the monkey on, around the monkey's waist, and around the tiger's waist, till the monkey couldn't fall off. Then off they went to the place where Mr. Rabbit was still dancing on the elephant.

Mr. Monkey was just about to utter a profuse greeting when Grandfather Rabbit spoke first.

"Mr. Monkey! Mr. Monkey! If it isn't Mr. Monkey with one of my father's tigers at last! At last! Now, Mr. Monkey, that is fine! Just tie that tiger to the tree over here, and then go right back and bring the other six. My father lent your father seven tigers a generation ago, and I'm not going to wait any longer. If you don't bring the other six tigers quickly, I will gather my uncles and aunties, and brothers and cousins, and nieces and nephews, and we will come and destroy you and all your uncles and aunties, and brothers and cousins, and nieces and nephews. And——"

"Oh ho!" said the tiger to himself. "So that is your clever plan, Mr. Monkey! You are trying to use me to pay your father's debt, are you? We'll soon see if you will tie me up to the tree." And he turned and ran through the forest, under the bushes through the thicket, as fast as he could go, and the poor monkey was dragged through it all. He was tied on so tight, and he was dragged through so many bushes that ever since that time all Mr. Monkey's descendants have had small waists. Ever since that time too the elephants have been friends of the rabbits, and Mr. Rabbit became the most famous lawyer in all the jungle world.

.   .   .   .   .   .

After reading this story, I said to Peter, "In the folklore stories of the jungle people, does the rabbit always win his case?"

"Oh, yes, Thara," he answered. "In our jungle tales the rabbit is the most clever animal. If he acts as lawyer he always wins his case. If he acts as a doctor, his medicine always cures his patient. He was always a friend to those in trouble."

"Oh, he was!" I said thoughtfully.

"Yes."

"Do you know, Peter," I added, "I have also found out that there is no difference in Karen between a hare and a rabbit."

"No, Thara, that's right."

"And so to the Karens I am Dr. Rabbit!"

"Yes, that's right, Thara."

"That's fine, Peter," I continued. "Dr. Rabbit—Thara Pa Deh it shall be." And from that time the labels on my eyedrops, tincture of iodine, castor oil, fever mixture, and ringworm lotion all had a little picture of a rabbit on them, and, whether that had anything to do with it or not, our dispensary began doing big business selling Bunny Brand medicines.

"Doctor, doctor, have you got any fry-smell medicine," said a poor old man one day as he held up his hand with a big boil on it.

"Fry-smell medicine," I said. "What kind of medicine is that?"

"Something to drink," he explained, "that will gather all the fry smell out of my hand so that my hand can get better."

"But what has fry smell got to do with that boil on your hand?" I asked.

"Well, you see, doctor, about ten days ago I was cutting bamboo in the jungle, and a piece of bamboo slipped across the back of my hand and cut it. It didn't bleed very much because I picked up a handful of dirt to rub into it, and it would have been quite all right, but that night, when I got home, the neighbor was frying a chicken, and that fry smell came into my nose, went down into my stomach, came up my left side, and down my left arm, and that night my hand began to throb and throb. The next day it got bigger and bigger and redder and redder till now look at all the fry smell in my hand."

I looked and smiled, "I've got something that will cure your fry smell all right," I assured him. Then slipping a little lance up my sleeve, I came out with a swab of iodine and painted the boil all over.

"Uncle, look at the little bird over there on the tree," I cried.

While he was looking for the little bird, I lanced his boil. He felt me cut it, and turned around. There was the pus running down into the basin, yellow and brown and green, with a terribly bad odor. His eyes sparkled, and he said joyfully, "There it goes! There it goes!"

"What goes?" I asked.

"The fry smell!" he exclaimed.

He thought that the pus was coagulated fry smell, and he said, "Now my hand will get better, won't it?"

"It surely will," I agreed, and in a few days that delighted man went up and down the country, telling everybody that he met, "If ever you get the fry smell, go down to the doctor at Ohn Daw. He's got the last word on fry smell. He's the fry-smell specialist."

I used to waste a lot of time trying to discount the fry-smell theory of infection and prove the germ theory, but they couldn't see germs, and lest I mar the effectiveness of my F.S.S. degree, I renamed iodine—"fry-smell medicine," and proved to everybody's satisfaction that Dr. Rabbit's fry-smell cure was the best.

"Doctor, doctor," called the chief fisherman from Kawkeyet as he came down the trail with seventeen of his servants, "I've got a tooth that I want pulled out," and as I looked up I caught the picture of a man who expected to have a big operation and had brought his seventeen servants to assist. Always willing to oblige, and having pulled hundreds of teeth since the first one fell out with the vibrations, I decided not to disappoint him, and welcomed him as one chief would welcome another. I brought him in, gave him my best mat, then stood his seventeen servants all around the room. To one I gave a towel, to another the absorbent cotton, to another a bundle of bamboo swab sticks. Another held a glass of water, another the permanganate crystals. Still others held the oil of cloves and the lance and the forceps on trays a little farther down the line

80

until every man had something to hold. I then took up my position in front of my patient and called for the man with the cotton and the man with the sticks to step forward. I made a swab very carefully and then called for the oil of cloves. That man stepped forward and dipping the swab I painted the tooth with oil of cloves.

"That's hot, isn't it, Uncle?" I said.

He nodded. I then put a few permanganate crystals in the glass of water, asked the man with the towel to stand at the right and the man with the basin to stand at the left, had the man with the forceps step forward, then took them with a flourish and fastened them on the tooth. It was so loose I could have pulled it with my fingers, but that would never have done. I was just about to pull the tooth when the dear old man suddenly found out that the oil of cloves had taken the pain from his tooth. He thereupon decided not to have the tooth pulled that day but instead to buy a bottle of this hot medicine and paint his tooth with that. Quickly lifting his hands he caught mine to stop me from pulling till he could explain, but the tooth was so loose that the jerk pulled it right out. I gave it to the man with the towel and, while the permanganate water and the basin were serving their purposes, told him to dry the tooth in the sun, tie a string around it, and hang it behind the door to remind him always of the Ohn Daw dispensary. That man went everywhere saying that the jungle doctor at Ohn Daw was the greatest dentist that ever walked the earth.

Thus God used our little dispensary and what little skill we had as one of the most effective tools in digging for our treasure, and the news of the God worshipers and their disease house went farther and farther throughout the land of the haunted pagoda.

School opened the next year with sixty-three students A third teacher was added to our staff, and we were still busy with the opening arrangements when Hte Po, the headman of La Po Ta village, eighteen miles across the hills to the west of Ohn Daw, put in his appearance with the startling request: "Thara, we want a teacher at La Po Ta. We are ready to open a school, and we want a Christian teacher."

Our friendship with Hte Po had been quite an inter esting one. He had come several years ago for a bottle of medicine. He had an attack of fever and had taken all the medicine the village doctors knew how to make. He had been bewitched in case his Kala (spirit) had gotten lost. He had been prayed for by the Buddhist priest, but nothing did him any good. Then he had heard of the God worshipers' disease house and had come for a bottle of medicine. That medicine, wrapped in a tract, made him better and kept him well for a whole year. Then he had another attack of fever. Another bottle of medicine, however, and another tract had kept him well for the second year. The third year we sold him a little book *Enemies of Health,* and he turned up soon after that with the joyful news that he hadn't smoked since reading that book. Evangelist Tha Myaing, having spent several weeks with him, had reported a fine interest, and we were now very happy indeed to hear that they wanted a teacher.

"But, Hte Po," I said, "we have no teachers ready yet It takes a long time to train teachers, and we would like them to have three more years in our training school at Meiktila after finishing up here."

"That doesn't matter, Thara," he replied. "We don't need a teacher like that. Here, give us Ohn Bwint, that big boy over there. He'll do. We know him. We see him go, we see him come, and we know he's a true man. We want Ohn Bwint."

"Ohn Bwint!" I repeated after him, and looked over to where a splendid young man was at study. "They want Ohn Bwint," I mused to myself, and for a minute or two I thought back over the four years Ohn Bwint had been in school. His father dedicated him as a boy to a Buddhist monastery. He had been there from the age of twelve to eighteen. There he had passed four grades of Burmese reading, writing, and arithmetic. He had worn the yellow robe, and after his first seven years of apprentice priesthood was just about to enter upon another seven years, when away off in his village, thirty-eight miles away, he heard of the God worshipers' mission station at Ohn Daw. The thought of people that were curseproof so aroused his curiosity that he decided to come to the mission school to study English. I'll never forget his first year at school. Wherever you saw him he had a habit of looking—looking. In the dispensary every chance he got he looked into the cupboard, under the tables, in the instrument cases. One day in my office I chanced to pull out one of the drawers to my desk while he was there. Down went his head to look. He looked into the phonograph, he looked into the piano, he looked under our bed, he looked in the kitchen. If ever we asked him what he wanted he answered politely, "Nothing. I'm just looking."

One day I called him to help me calk a seam in the motor launch, which was leaking a little. As I pulled up a couple of the floor boards, Ohn Bwint realized for the first time that the floor of the launch was not the bottom of the boat. Here was another hole for him to look into, and dropping

83

down upon his knees he peered under the floor and then cautiously groped in the hole with his arm.

"Ohn Bwint," I said laughing, "you *are* looking for something. Tell me what it is."

He looked at me a moment and then said, "Thara, don't be angry with me, but please tell me where do you keep your *dawtaka?*"

"Why, Ohn Bwint, we have no *dawtaka!*" I replied.

"But my mother says you have, Thara! At first she said you were the *dawtaka,* and then, when you didn't eat anybody up, she said that you had one kept secretly somewhere, and when I came down to school she told me not to give heavy sleep to my eyes till I had found the place where you keep it, and, Thara, I've looked and looked and looked, but I can't find it."

"Ohn Bwint," I said kindly, "you have my permission to look everywhere, but you will find no *dawtaka,* for there is no such thing," and from that day Ohn Bwint was a different boy. It seemed as if a heavy burden had fallen off his shoulders. The next school year he brought several more big boys to school with him, and now, after four years, he had just been baptized with seven other fine young men, the first fruits of our schoolwork.

Now Hte Po, the headman of La Po Ta, wanted Ohn Bwint for their village teacher! Going over to where he sat studying, I said, "Ohn Bwint, Hte Po wants you to open a school in La Po Ta. Do you want to go?"

"Thara, *I* cannot say," he replied earnestly. "If you think I can do the work, *you* tell me to go."

"I'm sure you can do the work, Ohn Bwint, but it's quite a poor district out there. The nearest store is eighteen miles away and ——"

84

"But, Thara," he broke in, "I'm not thinking of what I'm to eat. If they need me and if I can do the work, I will be happy to go."

"I know you will, Ohn Bwint, but you will be lonely out there. You will get your letters only once in three months."

"But that doesn't matter, Thara."

"And their houses are not very good. I don't know what kind of living quarters they will give you."

"Don't! Don't say any more like that, Thara," he said. "Didn't you tell me yourself that when Jesus came to work for us He said, 'Foxes have holes, and the birds of the air have nests; but the Son of man hath not where to lay His head'! I'll have some place to put my mat to lie down and sleep. If they can find something to eat, I can eat too. If only you think I can do the work."

That was the only burden on his heart, so off he went with Hte Po to open our first outschool. This was the next natural step in the development of our mission station. The year previous to this we had tried to open an outschool in Tiger Village, but the influence of the Buddhist priests at Kawmaley had divided the village, and they finally sent a delegation asking me not to attempt opening a school there, as the Buddhists were so angry that they would burn the school down.

Now, with our first outstation established, we could look forward to opening many more. Ohn Bwint did very faithful work and, at the end of that year he came to our little camp meeting with five bullock wagons loaded with people, and Chief Hte Po was ready for baptism. As we had expected, the eyes of the village folk everywhere were on this school, and next year we were able to open two more out-

85

schools, one twelve miles up river at Tha Kwe Kla, and one sixty miles down the river at Kawmaraung.

During Ohn Bwint's second year at La Po Ta something happened which will always be remembered for showing his true character. In establishing these outschools we recognized the value of calling the teachers together for regular workers' meetings, where experiences could be compared and studied, and suggestions could be made. We made these meetings coincide with the end of the quarter, so that, as the teachers assembled, the quarterly reports could be brought in also. It soon became the recognized rule that we hold a workers' meeting for our district on the first Sunday in each new quarter.

From two hundred to two hundred and fifty inches of rain are recorded in the Salween Valley each year. This flood of water falls between May and October. As long as it rains only one or two inches a day, traveling between villages is in no way impeded, because the country is built with deep river and creek beds to carry the water off, but when it rains four or five inches a day for a week, the country fills up, rice fields are covered, and everybody stays home for two or three weeks till the flood goes down.

Now it happened that the end of the third quarter of Ohn Bwint's second year at La Po Ta came at the peak of the flood. Though we hoped that the water would go down to enable us to have our workers' meeting, it rained and rained and rained. Then, as if to increase the impossibility, I received a telegram from Rangoon, calling me to a union committee meeting on Thursday, and it added, "Try to bring your reports with you."

I quickly called Peter and studied the situation. The boys wouldn't be coming in to the main station till Sunday.

Since the telegram gave us only two days to gather the reports before I must go to the city, we sent two of the boys up to Tha Kwe Kla by motor launch, and two more by river steamer down to Kawmaraung. Then taking one of the big boys with him, Peter tried to get out to La Po Ta. By the next evening they had all returned with their reports except Peter.

"It's no use, Thara, we couldn't get there," he explained. "Between here and the foothills there was six miles of water and mud, sometimes knee deep, sometimes up to our armpits, which we managed to get through. When we got to the foothills, however, we found a raging mountain torrent in every little valley. We swam across four of them, but the fifth was so deep and so wide that we couldn't get across. We waited all night, but as the water didn't go down, we couldn't get Ohn Bwint's report."

"Don't worry a minute," I hastened to encourage him. "Never mind the report! Your life is worth much more than a piece of paper. Ohn Bwint will never get in on Sunday, and we will mail his report sometime later on."

Accordingly, with all my reports but one, I went down to Rangoon on Thursday and attended the committee meeting the next day. I spent the Sabbath with the English church in the city, then on Sunday and Monday occupied my entire time in the bazaars. You can well imagine that, when we make these trips only three or four times a year, there is considerable shopping to do.

Monday afternoon, with my list all finished and my goods stored at the railway station, I came back to the mission headquarters to rest an hour or two before the train left that night.

As I came in, the superintendent greeted me. "Here's a

letter for you, Mr. Hare. Looks as if it's from your good wife."

A chill came over me, for so often unexpected letters brought news of the children being sick or something just as bad, but I soon began to smile as I read, "Everybody is well. I have just thought of a few more things we need and hope this will reach you in time."

Then followed a list of needles and thread, buttons and pins, and a lot of other things that didn't grow on our mission station. I looked up at the superintendent and said, "Everything is all right. It's just a little supplementary shopping list," and was just about to fold my letter up and put it in my pocket when I noticed there was a postscript. Quickly I read it; then my eyes filled with tears and my throat choked, for I read, "Ohn Bwint came in on Sunday according to the regular program. He had to swim across twenty rivers and walk through six miles of mud and water to his armpits, *but he brought in his report on time.*"

"Is there something the matter?" asked the superintendent as he noticed my emotion.

I passed the postscript over for him to read, and said, "We're finding treasure. We've just dug up a shining diamond, for I don't care whether that faithfulness is found in the heart of a white man or a black man or a brown man or a yellow man, that's the stuff God makes shining diamonds out of for His kingdom."

That was several years ago, and Ohn Bwint is still in La Po Ta. Although the following account really belongs nearer to the end of the story, I'll record it now while the memory of this brave boy is still fresh in your mind.

Just a few months ago I received a letter from him, and in it he said, "You'll be glad to know, Thara, that I am still in La Po Ta, but I am not village teacher any more. I am in charge of the district, and my first little school of ten or eleven children has grown to three village schools. We have just baptized the fifth person for this year, bringing our total baptisms in this district up to fifteen."

Then in his letter he told me one of those stories sweet to the ear of every missionary. In a village about three miles away there lived a very prosperous farmer, so prosperous that he was able to hire elephants to drag logs, and carpenters to saw them into boards and build him a wooden house. At the end of his veranda he built a huge spirit altar, and there before each meal a handful of rice was placed, the gong sounded, and the prayers uttered. Seven children were born, and because they believed their prosperity was due to their faithfulness in sacrificing to the devils, they sacrificed and prayed all the more. In the days of their prosperity Ohn Bwint often passed by and invited them to meeting, but they were too busy to listen, too busy ringing their gong and praying to the evil spirits. But one day calamity came. One of their children sickened and died, then another, and another, and another. Then two more, leaving only one little babe alive. On top of all this sadness and sorrow, the mother's eyes grew dim, and she went blind. Said Ohn Bwint to himself, "In the days of their prosperity they wouldn't listen, but now maybe in their sorrow they will be glad for the comfort of God"; so he called to see them.

The little blind woman was right in the midst of a sacrifice, but the old man listened and appreciated all that Ohn Bwint said. After a word of prayer to the living God, he shook Ohn Bwint warmly by the hand and said, "Come again! Come again."

Ohn Bwint went again, but still the little blind woman

sacrificed, and only the man would listen, but, when it came time to pray, he called his wife and said, "Hey woman! You pray loud and long to your devils, but they do you no good. We are going to pray to the living God. Come and join us. See what it feels like to pray to the God worshipers' God!" and simply out of curiosity she groped her way to where they sat, and listened while Ohn Bwint prayed. When he was done, her heart was touched, and she put out her hand and said, "Come again. Come again, won't you!"

Ohn Bwint went again and again and again, and then one day the old man said, "You are a teacher. You go, you come, you travel north and south, east and west. Someday you may find a doctor who can operate on my wife's eyes. If ever you do, remember me."

Ohn Bwint didn't say which doctor he found to perform the operation but after the blind eyes had been operated upon and the cataracts removed, in a few days, as soon as the bandages were taken off, the woman could see. She jumped up and down with rejoicing and called out,"I was like a dead person. I was in the grave. I was a slave of the evil spirits, but they were no good. I worshiped them all my life, but they took away my children, and then smote me with blindness. But in the darkness I found God, and now I'm alive again, but this time I live not for the devils but for the living God."

She began to come to Sabbath school, and in a few months Peter went up and baptized her—and that's the way we dug for our treasure.

With the spread of our work to the villages and out-stations, the need of training our big boys to do evangelistic work became more and more pressing. We sent a request to the division for help, and we rejoiced before long to have

Brother and Sister Harold Baird, of Australia, join our mission family. They were both trained nurses, and their presence at Ohn Daw enabled me to give more attention to the village work. As soon as school was out that year, I selected fifteen of my biggest boys and planned a preaching trip to all the villages near the riverbank, as far north as the Keido rapids, which make the upper Salween unnavigable to through traffic. We carried a big box of medicines to care for the sick, a stereopticon outfit, which used a gasoline lamp, to show pictures on the life of Christ at night, and, of course, I took my trumpet with me to help gather the people together. When we reached a village, our plan was to visit every house, treat the sick, and advertise our night meeting. Sometimes when we found two villages close together we would work them as one, and at night when the music would start, everyone would come. We would sing, tell the story of the fall of man and the life of Jesus the Saviour, and then sit around the campfires and talk to the old men about the God of their folklore poems. The boys thoroughly enjoyed it, and after one or two meetings we broke the story into two or three sections and had the boys do the preaching. Often, as I would see these boys doing their part so well, my heart would be full to overflowing to realize that a few years ago they were just the same as the unlovely devil worshipers they were now preaching to.

One evening a crowd of about two hundred had gathered around. Their approval and appreciation were expressed by happy grunts and much talking. When I began to show the pictures and tell the story, they continued their chorused Oh's and Ah's and Um's, which showed that they understood the words and enjoyed the pictures. I could not help picking out among their happy grunts of pleasure,

91

however, what sounded like a cry of pain, "Oh-h, Ah-h." I noticed that it came from the same direction each time, and it continued all through the meeting. It so distracted me that I intended to find out just what it was all about, but I found out much sooner than I expected.

We had just dismissed the meeting, and I was standing near some of the old men when through the crowd there came a blind man feeling his way toward me, guided by my voice as I spoke to the men. On reaching me, he took me by the arm, shook me as a cat shakes a rat, then screamed into my ear, "Why didn't you come two years ago! Why didn't you come two years ago! I could have seen the pictures then, but now I am blind, and I can't see anything. Oh-h, Oh-h!" he sobbed, "Why didn't you come two years ago!"

We tried to speak words of comfort and cheer to that poor old man, but his words still ring in my ears, "Why didn't you come two years ago!" and spur me to greater service.

As we returned to the mission station after that successful trip, we determined to repeat that program till every village within a hundred miles of us had heard the story. The joy of digging for the real treasure had almost made us forget the pile of silver bricks that was supposed to be buried somewhere underneath our own haunted pagoda. No terrible sounds ever struck our ears, no piercing shrieks or groaning ever disturbed our slumbers. Some of the children now and then declared that they saw the ball of fire hovering over the old ruins, but we didn't worry about it at all. Then one day as I sat in my office an old man stood looking at me through the window. I smiled at him and asked if he wanted some medicine.

"Oh, no, no!" was all he said.

"Would you like to come in and visit for a while?" I suggested.

"Oh, no, no!" he repeated.

"Maybe you have a boy here at school?"

"Oh, no, no!"

"Maybe you would like to listen to the phonograph?"

"Oh, no, no," he still replied, but he came closer and leaned on the window sill as he whispered, "Thara, can I just take a walk around your back yard?"

"Of course you can, Uncle! Just go right at it," I smiled, then, as he moved off, I turned to my secretary and said, "Tun Maung, you take a little walk around the back yard, too, for a little while and see what this man has up his sleeve. You know, Tun Maung, there are all kinds of men in the world, and we can never be too careful."

Tun Maung disappeared with a smile on his face, and in about ten minutes returned with a still bigger grin.

"What's the big secret?" I asked.

"He's coming right away, Thara. He will tell you," he said.

The old man followed him in, took the chair I offered him, shook his head sadly, and said, "Thara, I can't find it. I can't find it."

"Can't find what?" I asked sympathetically.

"The coconut palm," he said.

"But, Uncle, there must be a hundred of them. Look!" and I pointed out the window.

"Yes, I know, Thara, but I don't mean those. I mean the one over near the old pagoda."

"Oh," I smiled, "there never was a coconut palm over there."

"Oh, yes, there was," he answered, and drawing his chair closer so that he could whisper, he said, "My grandfather was one of the young men who helped to build the old Ohn Daw pagoda. He saw the treasure buried. It was a footprint of Buddha in marble, such as is usually buried underneath pagodas, and it was enshrined in a little room of silver bricks. But it was not buried under the pagoda, Thara. It was buried between the pagoda and the coconut palm on the riverbank. Of course, it would have been a terrible sin for my grandfather to dig it up, because he helped to bury it there, but when he died a few days ago he told me how to measure between the pagoda and the palm tree. You see I could be just digging a well or something like that, see, and find it accidentally, you know! But the coconut palm isn't there now."

"And I have never seen one there," I added.

"So," he went on, "I don't know what to do." He sat thinking for a while, then asked, "Thara, would you give me permission to come and dig up your back yard?"

"Well," I said, "if you found any treasure, what would my share be?"

"Oh, I hadn't thought of that," he faltered.

"Well, I have," I assured him.

He thought a moment longer. "Look, Thara," he said, holding up three fingers, "there will be my brother and me doing the digging and you giving permission. I will give you a third share."

"Agreed," I said. "Start tomorrow!"

"No! No! No! Tomorrow is not a lucky day, Thara. I have already divined with the chicken bones, and I'll come the twentieth day of your next month," and having said that, he rose and disappeared through the door.

94

5

More Precious Than Gold

><><><><><><><><

"More to be desired are they than gold,
yea, than much fine gold." Psalms 19:10.
"I will make a man more precious than fine
gold; even a man than the golden wedge
of Ophir." Isaiah 13:12.

Just as the Log From the Devil Tree Rolled Into Place Brother Baird Cried Out With Pain

More Precious Than Gold

><><><><><><><><><

AS THE TWENTIETH of the next month came nearer, we began to dream of silver bricks—and maybe gold! What couldn't we have done with a lot of treasure just then. We had just rebuilt our well, and this time, since we knew how, it was seven feet across at the top and seven feet across at the bottom. It was forty-five feet deep, with five feet of living water at the bottom.

"If we get the treasure, Thara," said Peter in a burst of enthusiasm one day, "we can buy an engine, and pump water from the well to a tank and have the water laid on to our houses."

"And, if we get the treasure," I added, "we can buy a dynamo to be run by our engine when it isn't pumping water, and we can have electric lights!"

"And if we get the treasure we can buy a motorcar to run on the new road they are making to Papun."

"And, if we get the treasure ——" I was about to add one more treasure dream when I remembered that the twentieth of the month was still a day or two off, so changed my mind and only said, "But it's IF we get the treasure, Peter—IF."

At last the twentieth day of the next month came, the day that the adventurer's chicken bones had divined to be the lucky day to snatch the buried treasure from the clutches of the evil spirits and the curse, but the man didn't come. He didn't come the next month or the next. He *never* came, and we heard folks whisper that he died a very mysterious death! Did you ask why Peter and I didn't dig for it ourselves? Well, I'll tell you why.

In the first place, we felt that as Christian missionaries it was best for us to ignore all the superstition that surrounded us and not do anything that would risk making the Buddhists more angry with us than they were. In the second place, our hearts were set on the real treasure, more precious than gold or silver, and the cry of the poor blind man up the river, "Why didn't you come two years ago!" haunted us and urged us to use every available minute of our time in business for the King.

No, the man who said he would dig for the silver bricks near the haunted pagoda at Ohn Daw never turned up, but let me tell you what did happen a few weeks after.

Old Naw Kya Tee, the mother of Hla Kin, the first one to be baptized, came to me one day and said, "Thara, do you believe in curses?"

I smiled and said, "Christians are never afraid of curses, you know, Aunty, for curses have no power over Christians."

"I know, I know," she replied. "Hla Kin has told me, and Hte Po, the chief at La Po Ta, has told me that after they were baptized they had no more bad dreams and no

98

more fear. Ton Pey and Naw Too want to be baptized at next camp meeting, and they want me to worship God too, and I've been thinking if you baptize my children and baptize my house, maybe I'd better learn more about God and be baptized too."

"Wonderful! Wonderful! Aunty," I exclaimed with joy.

"And," she went on slowly, "it's no good getting baptized unless I can understand, and how can I understand if I can't hear the preaching? And how can I hear the preaching if I don't come? And how can I come unless 1 live somewhere near?"

"That's right, that's right," I encouraged. "And so?"

"And so I've been thinking to myself, why not build my new house just across the river; then I could come to Sabbath school and worship!"

"Splendid! Why don't you, Aunty! That would be fine," I urged.

"Yes, but, Thara, don't you know? Haven't you heard? Hasn't anyone told you about the curse of the Thirty-Three Pagoda Village? They say the headman buried a diamond in the heart of the great devil tree. They say it has killed two men already. They say no one dares live there, so I thought before I build my house I would ask you first if you believed in curses."

"Were you going to buy the land?" I asked.

"No, no, Thara. We jungle folk need not buy uncleared land in the forest. All we do is to get the headman's permission, then clear the land, plant our rice and our gardens, pay our taxes each year, and as long as we dig and plant, it is ours."

"Then build your house and plant your garden, Aunty," I said. "Never fear!"

99

"But the curse, Thara. Is there any Christian magic that can break it?"

"Yes! Yes! Of course there is."

Her eyes twinkled with delight. "I thought there was! I thought there was! Tell me, Thara, what do you do?"

I leaned over and whispered, "When your house is finished, before you live in it, we will bring all the children over from the school and we will sing; then we will read the Bible, and then we will pray to our God—we will tell Him that one who is looking for eternal life is going to live here, one who is tired of the darkness and the slavery of the evil spirits, and one who longs to be set free, is going to sleep here; then we will pray for Him to send His angels that excel in strength to encamp round about you. Then the curse will have no power over you."

"Is it as easy as that?" she cried as tears filled her eyes. "Then Ton Pey and Naw Too can live with me and work with me in the mornings and evenings, and go to school every day. Oh, Thara, it seems too good to be true. And will the curse never come?"

"Aunty, every morning before you eat, have Ton Pey or Naw Too read from the Golden Book and ask God to send His angels for another day; then the curse will never come."

Slowly she nodded her head and rose to her feet. "I must start right now," she said quietly, and was gone.

Within the next few days signs of activity were seen on the opposite bank of the river. Two or three men who were relatives of old Naw Kya Tee made a little clearing at the foot of the thirty-three little hills, to which they dragged posts and bamboos. When all was ready, everybody on the mission station big enough to work went over to a house-raising rally, and in two more days the house was done. Then, with beautiful and impressive simplicity, we gathered to dedicate that house and ask for it the protection of the angels. Every evening we saw the light twinkling and knew that Ton Pey and Naw Too were studying their lessons after the afternoon's work, and often at bedtime, if we listened, we could hear their voices clearly singing across the half mile of water—

> "When He cometh, when He cometh
> To make up his jewels,
> All His jewels, precious jewels,
> His loved and His own.
> Like the stars of the morning,
> His bright crown adorning,
> They shall shine in their beauty,
> Bright gems for His crown."

"And are you happy now, Naw Kya Tee?" I inquired a few weeks later, as she came across to Sabbath school.

"Yes, yes, Thara, but ——" she hesitated.

"But what?" I asked.

"But I'm going away for one more trip!"

"Going away? Going where?" I said quite amazed.

"To Ton Pey's father," she said quietly. "You see, Thara, he had a job at Papun when the trouble came, and when they drove me out, he's the one who sent me word to sell if I could, as he wouldn't show his face in the village again. But everything is so different now, Thara, and I'm going to tell him all about it. We want our daddy to come back and start all over again."

"God bless you, Aunty," I said. "We will pray that He will bring you safely back."

Sure enough, within a month Naw Kya Tee came to

church one day, her face just beaming. A stranger followed her in jungle fashion.

"It's Ton Pey's father," she said. "He's come. He's come."

During the weeks that followed we had many interesting talks with Ton Pey's father. He was a worker in gold and silver, a maker of earrings and charms, but in his old age he confessed he had not found peace, though he had sought it everywhere, in the worship of spirits, in the pagodas of Buddha.

"Of course, you haven't found it there," I told him one day, "because peace is the gift of God, and it comes when we know Jesus has forgiven our sins and has gone to prepare us a place in His Father's house, where there are many mansions."

"That's what Hla Kin says," he acknowledged, "and Ton Pey and his mother too."

"And it's true!" I added, "It's true. Uncle, why not ask God to give you that peace too?"

"Yes, but I'm not ready now," he said a little sadly. "Ton Pey's mother says I must give up my smoking and betelnut first. Then I will have peace, but, Thara, how can I do it now? These habits have bound me all my life!"

"But God has power to help you break the habit now," I urged. "Our God never slumbers or sleeps. We need not wait till the full of the moon as the Buddhists do to expect a blessing. The ear of our God is always open to our cry."

"But, Thara, you can't ——"

"Listen, Uncle, did you know old Pati Soo Sa at Tha Kwe Kla?"

"Oh, yes, very well."

"Well, not long ago he came to me with a broken

thumb. He had neglected it till the broken end was black and dead, and I could see that the only thing that I could do was to cut it off. I pleaded with him to let me do it, but he was afraid. I told him of other fingers I had cut off and of little Mg Kwe's arm that I had cut off right below the shoulder. He's the little boy at Kawkeyet who fell off a load of wood, you remember?"

"Yes."

"But he was still afraid. I showed him my lance and my medicine for taking the pain away, and I begged him to let me do it then, but he was still afraid, and he said, 'Not now, Thara. First let me go back and try the witch doctor's medicine, and in about ten days, if it's not better, I'll let you cut it off.' I waited, but he never came back. 'Where's Uncle Soo Sa?' I finally inquired of some other patients who had come from Tha Kwe Kla. 'The old man with the broken thumb.' 'Oh,' they said, 'he's dead! He died three days ago.'"

I waited for a moment for the illustration to do its work, then asked, "Do you think he died because his thumb was broken?"

"Oh, no! no! Thara," Ton Pey's father replied. "He died because he wouldn't let you cut it off."

"And I had the power and the time and the medicine to do it that day when he came."

The old man sat silently looking into the fire. "Uncle," I said, "let us pray God to deliver you and give you peace now."

He nodded his head, and we prayed.

At our next camp meeting Naw Too and Ton Pey were baptized, and their father and mother followed them in this step a little later. For many months the little light gleamed

103

from the bamboo house across the river at the foot of the thirty-three little hills.

That little light shone over the hills to Tiger Village two miles away, and the first I knew of it a delegation of village elders called on me and said, "Thara, we're ready for our village school now!"

"You are?" I asked in surprise.

"Yes, we're ready now."

"But only two years ago you said you'd burn the school down."

"We know, Thara, we know. But for two years we have looked at La Po Ta. For two years we have seen your teachers go and come, and they are true men. Where they teach, light shines in the darkness. The sick get better, and they are not afraid anymore. We cannot wait any longer. We want a school now."

"But I have no money to build a school now," I reluctantly replied.

"We have built the school already. Naw Kya Tee told us to. She often comes to our village and talks to us. She said she knew if we built the school you would send the teacher."

"But my money is all divided already for this year," I replied. "Maybe I'll try to do something for you next year."

"Never mind the money, Thara. Give us a teacher. We will feed him and give him a basket of rice for each child we send to school."

"Rather poor wages," I said to myself, but to them I said, "Do you think you could coax a boy to go for that?"

We had been talking at the dispensary, and before those words were all out of my mouth, "Thara, Thara!"

104

someone called from the inpatient's ward. I passed quickly to the room and saw that it was one of my fine big lads, Mg Thein, who was still in quarantine after measles. "Please, Thara, won't you let me go?" he begged. "You know I've just finished school here, and I did hope to go to Meiktila to the training school. But, Thara, I can't make it now. Can't I go to Tiger Village?"

"Did you hear the wages they will pay, Mg Thein?" I asked.

"Never mind the wages, Thara. I'm after real gold as you are."

So Mg Thein went to Tiger Village, and about twenty-two boys and girls came to his little school there.

Among these little heathen boys and girls was one little ten-year-old boy named Very Tall. He must have been quite a long baby when he was born, for jungle mothers usually give character names to their children. You and I might think that Longfellow would have been a more suitable name. His mother, however, wasn't thinking of him lying down. She was thinking of him standing up, so she called him Very Tall. This little lad lived in a village four miles away, but in order to come to school he was staying with an uncle in Tiger Village. He had only been at school a few weeks when he saw something yellow that shone like gold in his teacher's Bible.

"What's that, Thara?" he asked.

"That, my boy, is a Sabbath school bookmark," was the answer. "Everybody who studies his Sabbath school lesson every day for a year and goes to Sabbath school every week for a year gets a beautiful golden ribbon like that."

"Do they?" said Very Tall, his eyes widening with wonder. "And if I study my lesson every day and go to

105

Sabbath school every week for a year, can I get one too?"

"You certainly can," Mg Thein assured him.

"Then that's what I'm going to get," he said emphatically, "a golden ribbon that shines like the golden streets of the New Jerusalem."

He started in to learn to read, and at the end of the first complete quarter he received a quarterly honor card, with two seals on it, signed by the superintendent. At the end of the second quarter he received another one, and the next quarter he received his third. Then he entered upon the fourth quarter, studying his lesson every day and counting the weeks away till he should receive his golden ribbon.

"Only five more Sabbaths. Only four more Sabbaths ——" and then one day a messenger came from his village. He came silently up the stairs into the schoolhouse, sat down, leaned over, spread the bamboo a little apart and spat out his betelnut. Then leaning over and touching Very Tall on the shoulder, he said, "Very Tall, ye'r mother's awful sick. Yer got to go home an' eat the devil worship," and Very Tall sat heavyhearted and sad all the rest of the school period. He loved his mother, and he liked going back to his village. It wasn't that, but how could he keep up his perfect record over in his village? There wasn't a Bible or anybody who could read in all the village. There wasn't a Christian anywhere near. What could he do? And there were only three more Sabbaths to the ribbon!

Quietly and sadly he sat thinking and wondering as he watched the children run out to play after school was dismissed, and then all of a sudden an idea struck him. He jumped down the school ladder, ran down the trail through the mango trees, and raced up the ladder to his teacher's room.

"Thara!" he panted. "Thara, I've just thought, haven't you got two Bibles? And couldn't you lend me one? Because there is not a single Bible in all my village. But, Thara, if you would lend me one of yours, I'd be so careful of it. I really would, Thara then I could keep up my record, and I'd have Sabbath school all by myself. Please, Thara ____"

"Of course you may have my extra Bible, Very Tall," said Mg Thein, and turning down the pages where that week's lesson and the next week's lesson were, he handed it to Very Tall, who put it under his jacket next to his little heart. Then, waving good-by to his teacher, he climbed down the ladder and disappeared down the trail through the bamboos, calling out, "I'll be faithful, Thara! I'll be faithful!"

Mg Thein's heart bounded with joy as he saw the little fellow go, and he stood there for a moment enjoying the thrill that comes to everyone who realizes that God is using him to make others faithful. Then he turned to prepare his evening meal. He lit a fire, put on a pot of rice to cook, and reached into the basket on the wall for some vegetables to put in the stew to eat with his rice. The basket was empty, but that didn't matter. There were plenty of things in the jungle to cook, all he had to do was to go and get them. Swinging the basket onto his back, he took down the big knife that hung near it on the wall, and set off down the same trail that Very Tall had taken a little while before. Mg Thein did not walk quickly. He was not going to any particular place. Looking for roots and leaves and bamboo shoots, he walked slowly, turning now to the

107

right to pick some leaves, now to the left to dig a root. Before going very far, he came to a small clearing in the bamboos and found Very Tall right there, sitting under a tree. He was surprised, to say the least. But when he saw Very Tall smuggle something under the corner of his jacket, hang his head as if in shame, while his ears and face went red, he was alarmed! He stood still, thinking fast, as Very Tall slowly rose and came toward him.

"Why that look of guilt?" thought Mg Thein. "Why those red ears and that red face?" and there seemed only one solution to him. "I know, I know," he groaned in his soul. "Very Tall, you've been smoking. I suppose as you came past yonder devil altar and saw the tobacco that you couldn't resist the temptation. Oh, Very Tall, oh, Very Tall."

By this time, however, Very Tall was close enough to speak, and with his head still hung in shame and embarrassment, he said in a loud hoarse whisper, "Thara, Thara, will God be angry with me—for—for reading the Bible in the jungle?"

"For what? What have you been doing?" said Mg Thein in excitement.

"Reading the Bible in the jungle," repeated Very Tall.

"Oh, Very Tall, is that what you have been doing? I thought—I thought—er—is that what you have under the corner of your jacket? No! No! God is not angry. He loves us to read the Bible everywhere," said Mg Thein, much relieved in spirit.

"You see, Thara," Very Tall hastened to explain, "I began to wonder what I would do if I came to a word that I couldn't read, because there's no one in my village who can read, and it would be too far to come back and ask you,

108

so I thought I had better read it before I went home, and it's all right, Thara, I can. There aren't any words too hard, and I've read all this week's and all next week's lesson, Thara, but will God be angry?"

Mg Thein patted him on his back, assured him again that God would not be angry, then, with a smile on his face, putting the Bible back in its place near his little heart, he turned, and waving good-by sped along the trail, calling out as he disappeared, "I'll be faithful, Thara. I'll be faithful."

Before long he was clambering up the ladder to his own bamboo house. His poor sick mother, lying on a mat near the fireplace, hearing him, raised her head and called to him in a weak, sickly voice, "Very Tall, I—see—you've come. Go—and tell—your father that you're here—and to —roast the pig—then tonight—when everybody is asleep —we will sacrifice—to the devils."

Obediently Very Tall ran and told his father, and that night, after everybody had gone to sleep, the father gathered his family around the roast pig in a very dim light and, while holding hands, prayed something like this:

"Oh, Devils. Oh, Devils,
Here's a pig for you. Here's a pig for you.
Don't be angry with us. Don't be angry with us.
Let mother get better. Let mother get better.
Oh, Devils. Oh, Devils."

They prayed and they waited, but the mother didn't get better. They waited for three days; then the sick woman said, "Husband, I don't think—the devil liked the pig. I think—he wants—a chicken."

So they went through the sacrifice all over again with a chicken. They prayed and they waited, but the poor, sick

109

mother didn't get better. Then she said, "Husband—I don't know—anything—more to do. We've had the—witch doctor—and the—bark and root—doctor. Now—we've had —the sacrifice twice, but—I'm no better."

"There's only one thing more, Mother," said her husband. "I've sent for the Buddhist priest, and he's coming in the morning to pray for you; then maybe you'll get better."

Early the next morning, heralded by two boys who banged a big brass gong that hung from a bamboo carried on their shoulders, the Buddhist priest came slowly into the village. As the gong sounded, the village folk, knowing just what it meant, all came and knelt by the path on which the priest would pass and, as he went by, they bowed down with their hands and their foreheads right to the ground. Did I say everybody? I should not have. I should have said everybody but Very Tall, for Very Tall stood straight and very tall, and did not bow one inch. He had learned at Tiger Village Mission school that we should worship only God, who made heaven and earth, and he purposed not to bow in worship before a man, but his poor sick mother saw him standing straight and tall. To her he was insulting the priest, and the straighter he stood the more angry she became, till at last she could not keep in her hot, bitter words any longer, but screamed out with what strength she had, "Bow down—you little—white-toothed dog. Bow down—you little—white-toothed dog. Can't you see—the priest—has come—to pray for me. Bow down— you little—white-toothed dog!"

Poor little Very Tall, I know how he felt that day. I've been called a white-toothed dog, and it doesn't make you feel very happy. He looked at his mother, and he looked at the priest, but while he was wondering just what to do,

110

his father slipped up the ladder and ran over to his wife, "Mother," he said quickly. "Never mind about Very Tall. Don't make him worship the priest. You know nothing has made you any better yet, and I've been thinking, maybe even the priest's prayers won't make you any better, and then, Mother, maybe Very Tall knows how to pray to the white man's God, and then maybe you will get better."

So Very Tall didn't have to worship the priest, but stood there watching as the priest slowly went up the stairs and seated himself behind a big palm-leaf fan. Then after lighted candles had been placed all around the patient, he prayed his monotonous Burmese prayer. He prayed and he prayed, but the poor sick mother didn't get any better. Then after a few days the father called Very Tall to him.

"We have tried everything we know, my son, and mother doesn't get better. I've been wondering, do you know how to pray to the white man's God?"

"Oh, yes, Father, I can. And we don't have to wait till everybody has gone to bed. We can do it now, Father. Get the children and kneel down and shut your eyes, and when I'm all finished say, 'Amen,' and then God will make mother better. I know He will, Father."

They gathered on their knees about the wondering sick woman while Very Tall prayed. "Please, Jesus, make mother better. They don't know you yet, and all their worship doesn't make her any better, but please, Jesus, won't you make her well so that they will know that you are stronger than all the evil spirits. For Jesus' sake, Amen."

It was with greatest difficulty that the father could say Amen, but he did the best he could do, as his voice choked with emotion. But the mother! As her little boy prayed, the little boy she had cursed so bitterly a few days before, her heart was moved as it had never been moved before. As the tears rolled down her face, she put out her hand and drew Very Tall to her and said, "Very Tall—my son—mother is feeling better already, she is. I think mother will be all better—soon."

The next morning she could sit up, and the next day she could stand up. Embracing her little boy, she said, "You must go back to school, Very Tall. Your lessons must not stop for too long, but when you get back, tell your teacher it wasn't the devil worship that made mother better, and it wasn't the priest's prayers that made mother better, but it was her own boy's prayers to the living God that made mother better."

Catching up his precious Bible, he hugged it to his heart, said good-by, and bounded down the ladder and along the trail through the bamboos and the little hills back to Tiger Village. Then, racing up to his teacher's house, he said, puffing and panting, "Please, teacher—be sure to mark me up with—two big sevens—because I read my lesson three times—every day and—on Sabbath I had Sabbath school all day long—so you'll be sure to mark my record with two big sevens, won't you, please, teacher!"

Of course his teacher did, and in a few weeks the beautiful yellow ribbon that shines like the golden streets of the New Jerusalem was placed in his hands, and a letter from Mg Thein said, "We're finding treasure too, Thara—treasure more valuable than gold."

The months that followed the opening of Tiger Village school were progressive months on the main station. Brother Harold Baird had proved to be one of the most

112

practical missionaries I have ever seen. He taught the boys to clear the land, to make bricks, to saw lumber, and build houses. One by one the logs of the mission property were sawn up; then other logs were dragged from the near-by forests and sawn up too. One by one the bamboo buildings gave way to strong, well-built structures of brick and wood. As the boys realized the glory of their efforts, our school spirit rose, and a hundred miles on every side of us, people heard of the wonderful school at Ohn Daw.

Then one day Brother Baird dropped into my office for a chat. "You know, Brother Hare, we need some new tables and desk tops for our school."

"That's a fine idea," I said. "When do you think you can get the lumber?"

"Well, that's just the trouble," he replied. "I've walked all around the jungle on this side of the river and I can't find a tree big enough anywhere. But have you ever noticed that big tree lying on the ground in Naw Kya Tee's rice field across the river?"

"The one that is about five feet through at the butt?"

"Yes, that one. It is thirty-three feet long before it branches and it is three feet through at the top. Now, if ____ "

"But, Thara Baird," I said. "Haven't you heard? Don't you know? Hasn't anybody ever told you?"

"Told me what?"

"Why, that's the old devil tree of the village of Thirty-Three Pagodas," I replied. "That's the tree that is supposed to have the diamond in it. Listen! Just after we established ourselves here in Ohn Daw, two men in a village five miles away said, 'The curse is broken now that the God worshipers have come. Let us saw down the tree, split it up for firewood, and find the diamond.' So they took a saw and began to saw the tree down, but before they were half-way through, one man cried out with pain. His friend took him home at once, but he died. No one else dared to touch it till Naw Kya Tee built her house over there, and Ton Pey said he was going to clear the land on the hillside for his rice field. He remarked, 'I don't think the spirits have any power over Christians, but all the same I'm not going to meddle with the old tree.' However, as he felled his trees and bamboos they fell toward the tree and, when the dry timber and bamboos had burned away, lo! the devil tree lay in the ashes. All the jungle people prophesied, 'Now watch him die!' but he didn't die. He planted his rice and reaped a bountiful harvest. Then two more people came with a saw. 'Ah,' they said, 'the curse is broken now. Let us saw up the log and find the diamond.' You'll see the cut they made up near the fork, but when they got halfway through, one of them cried out with pain, and they took him home, and he died."

"Oh, so that's the tree," said Brother Baird.

"That's the tree, and that's the story," said I.

"But it would make lovely table tops and desk tops, Brother Hare," he argued. "Look here. We're not afraid. You get a sawpit license for that side of the river, and I'll saw the thing up into boards."

So I applied to the government for the sawpit license, and in a few weeks Mr. Baird announced, "We have two lovely logs fifteen feet long, and we have built the saw pit just down the hill a few feet from where the logs are. We will have the first one on the skids today."

I watched the boys go over with him and heard a shout of triumph as the first log rolled into place on the sawpit skids, but it seemed only a second before I heard the launch engine start up and saw them all come home.

"What's the matter?" I shouted as the launch came alongside the landing. "What's the matter?" For answer they pointed to Brother Baird, who lay as white as death on the seat, groaning in pain.

"An accident?" I questioned.

"No, Thara, everything went all right. The log rolled down as nice as could be, but as soon as it came to its place on the skids, Brother Baird cried out with pain, and we have brought him home."

Tenderly we carried him to his house. Carefully I tried to diagnose his trouble, but already through the jungle they were whispering, "The devils have got him. The devils have got him. Now let us see who is the strongest. The white man's God or our devils!"

CHAPTER

6

Silver and Brass

>‹›‹›‹›‹›‹›‹›‹›‹›‹

"For from the rising of the sun even unto the
going down of the same My name shall be
great among the Gentiles; and in every place
incense shall be offered unto My name, and
a pure offering: for My name shall be great
among the heathen, saith the Lord of hosts."
Malachi 1:11.

The Greatest Accomplishment of the Band Was Breaking Down the Fear of the *Dawtakas*

6

Silver and Brass

>+>+>+>+>+>+>+>+>+

IN A FEW hours Mr. Baird was delirious, and his fever up to 105 degrees. "He had a chill last night," said Mrs. Baird. "I tried to persuade him not to go to work today, but you know how enthusiastic he is about those logs."

"A chill last night!" I echoed, and noted it on my chart. "Did he have any fever during the night?"

"Yes," she answered, "but he said he was all right this morning, so I just thought it was another attack of malaria."

We tried to give him a little medicine, but he could not retain it, so we treated him hypodermically, but the poor man was suffering greatly, and in spite of all our care and treatment he hovered on the brink of unconsciousness for three days. "Malignant malaria," was our verdict after careful observation for a few days, and we were quite sure of our diagnosis, but the jungle folk whispered, "The devils have got him," and watched.

How we prayed that God would give us the life of our brother, for it mattered little what we believed was the cause of his trouble. To them it was a conflict between their devils and the white man's God, and God's cause could not suffer defeat. As we prayed, the fever was rebuked, the pain eased, and by the tenth day he was able to get out of bed and take a trip to our rest home in the Shan Hills, where it took him three months to recuperate.

Then he was back with us again as hale and hearty as ever, and it was very gratifying to see the jungle folk wagging their heads and to hear them say, "Oh, well, of course the white man's God is stronger than our devils. Of course! Of course!"

Personally, I think that the other men died of malignant malaria also, but I have never tried to convince the jungle folk of that. They *know* it was the curse that killed them.

But I must tell you about the diamond. Because of the huge size of the logs, we hired some sawyers to help the boys, and one day after school was opened I heard a yell and a shout from across the river. The saw was going double speed. It sounded so interesting that I sped across the river in the launch to see what it was all about. There were the men as excited as could be, the perspiration just rolling off them, their eyes bulging with expectancy.

"What is it? What is it?" I shouted.

"We—came—to something hard," panted the man on top without slackening his speed. "It—may be—the diamond."

As I made more careful examination I could see that they had started the cut at one end of the log and, after going about one third of the distance, had stopped and started at the other end. Evidently they had struck something hard right there, and it might be the diamond, of course! Spirit worshipers did do fantastic things like that, though personally I had thought the diamond to be probably only the size of a grain of sand. However, the men were sawing frantically. They would soon be there. As there was no stopping them, I sat around awaiting the big moment. One foot more to go! I found myself blowing the sawdust from the line for them and putting the chocks on the skids to catch the half logs when the tree split open. I found myself holding the big wooden wedge and the hammer to help break the log open—for it might—it might be a diamond, a huge, big diamond. Of course, the men would get a share of the treasure, everybody would. One more inch to go! I heard it grate on the saw tooth!

"There it is," the men shouted as they more carefully tilted the saw to cut as far above and as far below the diamond as possible.

"Finished!" cried the man on top.

With a deft knock the lower man slid off the bottom handle while the top man pulled the saw through and hung it on a bamboo rafter of the roof above them. I placed the wedge in position, and after a few taps the great log snapped the remaining fibers that held it and rolled easily open onto the chocks. There it was—a lead bullet from a thirty-bore rifle that somebody had shot into the heart of that majestic tree. We looked for a moment in awed, disappointed silence, and then sat down and hee-hawed at ourselves. Hee-hawed to our heart's content. Of course, the diamond may still be there. There are many of the limbs and branches still left, but, when you come to hunt for the treasure, we will show you what we really got—the

121

new desk tops and table tops—valuable treasure from the devil tree.

That year we opened up two more outstations, one at Awbawa, a hundred miles away across the mountains to the west, the other at Kawdawko, thirty miles to the south. We now had eight Sabbath schools, with 292 students, two organized churches, with 130 baptized members, and our staff of twenty-one workers, pastors, teachers, nurses, and evangelists were busy all the time. As I fondly think of the evangelistic influences of this period, I believe that the most powerful was the treasure of silver and brass that we found. I will never forget the clue that started us digging for this treasure. It was away back when we began to teach the boys how to hold meetings and preach during our summer vacation trips. To be accurate, it was the third such preaching tour that we made, and in addition to my fifteen big boys, we were accompanied by Mr. L. W. Melendy, the union mission secretary, and Mr. Baird, my associate missionary. Both Mr. Melendy and Mr. Baird played cornets, so that in addition to our box of medicines for the sick people and the stereopticon outfit for the pictures at night, we had three brass instruments to help in the music. We outlined our trip to take in every village in the northeast section of our territory, which reached right over to the border of Siam. Day by day we were having inspiring meetings. All were enjoying the training and the experience as well as the gorgeous rugged scenery.

One afternoon we came to the most dilapidated, tumble-down village we had ever seen, called Parkete. Our boys took one glance at the houses and then said, "Well, we won't be having a meeting here tonight surely. There can be nobody living here."

The village truly was a discouraging sight. The houses were built of bamboo, but they were old, and the bamboo posts had rotted through. Many of the houses had already collapsed, and others were leaning dangerously, but I answered, "Well, boys, we'll go visiting first and see if anybody lives here. Even if there are only half a dozen, we'll have the meeting just the same. You won't be nearly so nervous talking to six people as you would if you had six hundred."

"Of course we won't, Thara," they replied; so off we went visiting, and we were astonished to find about twelve people around.

"Come on, boys," I said. "There are a dozen anyway, and maybe some more will come back by sunset."

Those wonderful boys set to work with a will, and by the time the sun began to sink in the west, the sheet was stretched on a bamboo frame and our picture machine all set up. Out came our three cornets, and we began to play. Say! You should have seen that village! It seemed to grow arms and legs everywhere. Out of those tumble-down houses they came, from behind their rice barns they came, from out of the shade of the giant trees and overhanging bamboos of the forest they came running—mothers and fathers, aunties and uncles, nieces and nephews, grandmothers and grandfathers—till there were over fifty of them at our meeting that night.

With intense satisfaction our boys watched them assemble, then said, "We know. We know. We know what did it. It's the trumpets! It's the trumpets!" as though our trumpets had the power to create men and women on the spot. In the next breath they added, "Thara, just imagine how wonderful it would be if every one of us had a trum-

pet!" and it was just then that I got the clue to the treasure
of silver and brass, for it was right there in that old tumbled-
down village of Parkete that there was born in my heart a
determination to have a brass band in the jungle someday, with every one of my preaching group owning a trumpet! I began to dream about it. I began to plan for it, and
in a year or two, when I found myself in Australia during
my first furlough, I found it quite easy as I was invited to
go from church to church and from college to college and
from camp meeting to camp meeting to talk about Burma,
to talk also about the boys in the jungle who wanted some
trumpets to help preach the gospel.

I soon discovered that the people in Australia had big,
warm, sympathetic hearts, and it wasn't long before one of
them said, "Mr. Hare, here's a trumpet. I haven't played
since I was a boy. You're welcome to it." Another man gave
me a trombone, another a euphonium, another a check to
buy a drum, and one by one we gathered the treasure of
silver and brass together. I was happy that my plan for a
band was to be realized.

Ernest Baldwin, one of my boyhood friends of Avondale
school days, said, "I'll show the pictures for you in all the
churches around Sydney, Bunny." He always called me
Bunny. Night after night, week after week, he gave up his
evenings at home to help me carry heavy equipment around,
and to tell the story in the suburban churches. It would
be nearly midnight by the time we had walked more than
a mile from the station to our homes in Wahroonga, but
his joy was to ask, "Well, how many does that make,
Bunny?" and night by night we counted our part of the
collections, night by night I told him of good bargains at
the secondhand shops, night by night I told him of gener-

ous gifts that had come through the mail, till at last we had twenty-three silver and brass instruments!

> We packed them in boxes—in iron-bound boxes,
>   And took them to Burma, a long way from home,
> To the boys in the jungle who wanted some trumpets,
>   To help preach the gospel where'er they might roam.

But just a minute, let me tell you a little secret! I've found out a great deal about brass bands that I didn't know before, and one thing is that you have to have something else besides silver and brass instruments before you can have a brass band, and if you don't believe me, you should have been there for our first band practice. How can I find words to describe that horrible occasion!

Those big boxes had been downstairs under our mission bungalow for a week before we started our band, because you can't open every box the first day you get back from your furlough. The boys had come every day to see if the boxes were open yet. I saw them put their ears down to them and listen. I saw them lift one end then another. I saw them knock this side and that; then one day I saw two boys slowly shake their heads as one said laconically, "No, there's nothing in 'em. There's nothing in 'em. If there was, it surely would have hatched by this time."

When their hope was at lowest ebb, one morning in chapel I read out the names of twenty-three boys whom I had selected to play the band, and announced the first band practice for noon that day. I never have been able to figure out just what happened to the clocks that day, but noon came about ten-thirty in the morning, and instead of twenty-three boys, I had about 153 for our first band practice. There was plenty of help to get the lids off. I took out the

first instrument, a big E flat bass, handed it to Ohn Bwint
and said, "Here you are, Ohn Bwint. Take the paper off
and see what you can do with this."

He took the paper off. That was easy. Then he stood
there looking at that great big horn. Since the only instrument he had ever seen before was my trumpet, he put it
up in trumpet position with the curved part near his face
and the bell poking straight out in front. But as it didn't
seem to fit that way, he stood it down on the floor with the
bell upward, put his head in the bell, and began to whistle.
That didn't do either, so he brought it over to me and said,
"Thara, I can't find the beginning of this thing. Where's
the beginning of it?"

I put my hand into the box, got the mouthpiece, and
showed him where the beginning of it was. Then I showed
him how to put his lips on it and how to put his arms
around it and how to wiggle his fingers up and down, and
soon I had him over in the corner, making horrible noises.

The next instrument to come out was a cornet. I handed
that to Baw Dee and said, "Here you are, Baw Dee. See
what you can do with this!" He did with it what he had seen
me do hundreds of times. He put the mouthpiece in—just
so, lifted the cornet to his lips, curled his little finger just
right, and began to blow. He blew and he blew, but it
wouldn't make a noise for him, so he blew a little harder
and wiggled his fingers up and down a little faster. He blew
till the perspiration rolled down his face and his fingers
were tired, but it wasn't any good. It wouldn't make a noise
for him, and, quite discouraged, he brought it to me and
said, "Thara, there's something the matter with this horn.
It won't sing for me." I showed him how to put his lips on
the mouthpiece and how to move his fingers up and down

properly, and soon he was in another corner, making more horrible noises.

Now multiply this performance by twenty-three, and you have our first band practice. Oh, how can I describe it! Poor Mrs. Hare upstairs! I heard her slam the back door, and, as she ran downstairs toward the jungle with her baby in her arms, she called out, "If that noise doesn't stop, I'll go crazy."

But don't worry. Mrs. Hare didn't go crazy. She's still all right, but I'll tell you what did happen. I went to bed that evening with an attack of malaria fever.

If ever you've had malaria, you know how the bugs stay in your blood, and as long as your body tone keeps up, they don't seem to worry you, but when through overexertion or exhaustion your body tone is lowered, well, then your malaria bugs begin to work and you begin to shiver and shake with ague, and soon you have a headache and high fever. Well, believe me, after three hours of that kind of band practice, I had all the exhaustion necessary for my malaria bugs to begin business, and that night I had a raging attack of fever. But in my fever there came one ray of hope. I said to myself, "Maybe this horrid noise is just the noise in my ears caused by the quinine, and maybe this brass band is just some kind of bad dream or nightmare that I am having, and when my fever gets better and my head stops aching, maybe I'll wake up to find that there isn't a brass band in the jungle at all."

But it wasn't a dream. It wasn't a nightmare. It was just as real as twenty-three flesh-and-blood boys could make it, and every morning, noon, and night they were downstairs under the bungalow, tooting those horns. On the third day I got out of bed and tried to tune them up, but it was no good. Those boys couldn't blow the same note twice, and I began to realize that I had on my hands the biggest proposition I had ever tackled in my life. I began to wonder whatever in the wide world I was going to do with twenty-three noisy brass horns in the jungle.

But let me tell you, those boys solved their own problem. They wanted so much to "play the band" to help preach the gospel to their own people that when they went to bed at night they fell on their knees and prayed, "Oh, God, help us to blow the band, so that we can help Thara preach the gospel," and the great God whom we love and serve, the God who has given white men wisdom enough to make these marvelous instruments, gave those humble jungle boys enough skill to play them. It sounds like a fairy tale, but just exactly four weeks from our first band practice, we were holding our first open-air meeting in a village near by. Why, no, we didn't play any difficult music. We played three little hymn tunes, but we played them again and again, and the jungle people said it was wonderful, and I think it was wonderful too.

As the jungle people flocked around, I saw a new day dawning for the preaching of the gospel. I can remember the time when singlehanded, with a bag of medicines, a Picture Roll, and my own trumpet, I had worked hard visiting every house, treating all the sick, and it took me three hours to gather twenty or thirty people together, but we don't have to do that way now. Oh, no! When we want to hold a meeting in a village now, the boys shine up their horns. Then we march to the center of the village and form the most wonderful shining ring you ever saw. The bandmaster steps forward, raises his baton, and says, "Boys, after two!" and after two the band starts. After two more

128

everybody in the village starts. They can't help it, and uncles and aunties, nieces and nephews, grandpas and grandmas, come running to hear.

"The band! The band!" you hear them call from one end of the village to the other. "Come on! The band!" and buffaloes and bullocks are forgotten, to roam where they will. The rice is forgotten and left on the fire to burn. Nothing matters when the band plays. By the time two to six hundred have gathered, according to the size of the village, we explain that it takes a lot of breath to play the band, and while we are catching our breath and getting ready for some music, one of the boys steps forward and tells the opening chapters in the life of Christ. Then the band plays some more, and another boy continues the story, and the band keeps playing and resting and playing and resting till the story of Jesus, the Saviour of the world, is told. Nobody leaves till the last note is played. We frequently begin our meetings as the sun is setting, and continue until nine-thirty or ten o'clock at night. Oh, yes, the preaching of the gospel among the devil worshipers has been revolutionized since we found our treasure of silver and of brass.

Of course, we have learned to play well as the months and years have gone by, and our playing of marches and waltzes is just as good as any academy band I have ever heard. Every morning before school opens the band plays for twenty minutes, ten minutes of which accompanies physical exercises and marching, which are part of the opening exercises of the school. These drills attract great crowds at times, and even our government officials, the district commissioner, and the forest officers go out of their way to enjoy them.

The greatest honor that ever came to the jungle band

was the invitation of Elder George Pettit, pastor of the English church in Rangoon, to come to the city for an Ingathering program. Boys who had never ridden on a "fire boat" or a "fire cart" before had their first ride on a steamer and a railway train, and in spite of a lost instrument, three lost tickets, and three boys getting malaria, our program was a great success and added three hundred rupees to the Ingathering fund. The Lord-mayor of Rangoon, who presided at our program, was highly complimentary and invited us to come again.

The greatest accomplishment of the band, however, was the breaking down of the fear of the *dawtakas*. The people simply could not be afraid when the band played.

We held annual meetings of four or five days each at all our outstations, and each year toured the villages in the territory of one or more of them. We walked literally hundreds of miles together up hill and down dale, and only eternity will reveal all the good the band has done. It has proved a great attraction for our annual camp meetings. I know the old chief told us the people would never come even if we did build a hospital or a school, because they were afraid of the curse of the Ohn Daw pagoda, but when the band played, they couldn't hear the groaning and screaming of the evil spirits, and the whole countryside came.

I remember that after four or five years of work we tried to hold our first camp meeting at the close of the school year. Thirty people came. We were greatly encouraged, but at our last camp meeting more than five hundred people came, and stayed the entire time. In the evenings our compound was filled with bullock wagons and our river-bank jammed with canoes, as from twelve hundred to fif-

130

teen hundred people came to our meetings each evening.

If you could have heard that great congregation, accompanied by the band, singing "What a wonderful change in my life has been wrought, since Jesus came into my heart"; if you could have heard them singing "In a little while we're going home," then you would have known that God had indeed chosen this place in which to make His name great.

"Thara, we don't need to go to heaven," said Kale Paw's grandpa as tears of joy streamed down his face. "This is enough. This is enough. I'm so glad my little grandson came to school. I'm so glad he gave his heart to God. You remember when Peter was in my village he taught me the truth, but I was bound with betelnut and tobacco, and I couldn't give them up. Even when you prayed with me and pleaded with me, I couldn't give them up, but when my little grandson, Kale Paw, wrote to me and said, 'Wouldn't it be lovely, Grandpa, if you and I could be baptized together,' I just had to give them up, and now, Thara, I'm so glad I did. I'm so glad we were baptized together. Surely heaven can't be sweeter than this."

"Aye! Aye!" chorused those who had gathered around as the dear old man spoke. "We didn't know how dark it was before till we saw the light. We didn't know what slaves we were before till we were made free. We didn't know how sad we were till our hearts were filled with the joy of Jesus."

But the powers of darkness were not willing to let the treasure go without a struggle, and they brought a flood to drown out the God worshipers. The waters covered the mission property and threatened the buildings, but the God worshipers sang "Bringing in the Sheaves" as they worked waist deep in water, bringing Evangelist Tha Myaung's goods and rice to the school building, which was on higher ground. The flood went down, leaving three inches of mud on the downstairs floor of the mission bungalow, but not a building was destroyed or a life lost.

Then the powers of darkness brought a tornado and took the roof off the mission bungalow. Roofing tiles and sheets of iron flew hither and yon, but when it had passed I found Mrs. Hare and the little ones downstairs sheltered under a table, singing "Jesus Loves Me; This I Know," and in a few days the roof was repaired stronger than ever.

An interested man brought his wife to our dispensary fevered and paralyzed with beriberi. In a week or ten days her fever was gone, and she was eating well, and we promised that in a few months her paralysis would improve. Then one morning her father brought a devil doctor, and after making charcoal figures on a bamboo tray and muttering all kinds of incantations, he solemnly announced, "The spirits have caught her *Kalar* (spirit), and they have it in a village thirty-eight miles away. She can never get better till she has eaten a sacrifice to the evil one and he lets her *Kalar* come back."

And in spite of my assurances and entreaties, they put her in a blanket, suspended it from a stout bamboo pole, and four strong men took two days to carry her to the village, thirty-eight miles away. When she got there she was nearer dead than ever. They had the devil sacrifice, but when she didn't rally, they called another devil doctor. He went through his incantations and said the diagnosis was right. The devils had her spirit, but it was in her husband's village, thirty-four miles back along the same road. They put her into the blanket again, but she didn't reach her hus-

132

band's village alive. She died on the way. We undoubtedly could have saved that life, but she was snatched away by the devils.

One summer I relieved the pastor of the English church while Mrs. Hare remained in the hill station a little longer with the children. We started back just in time for the opening of the school, traveling on the steamer up the great Salween River with forty-four boxes and bundles of cloth, schoolbooks, medicines, rice, lentils, and other supplies for our mission station. Arriving at Shwegun still twenty miles away, we were disappointed to find that our telegram had not been delivered, and there was no mission launch to meet us. We conferred with our evangelist Tha Myaing who was with us, and decided that he and I should walk through to the mission that night and bring the launch down the next morning before the return of the river steamer. Since it was only twenty miles away, we could easily walk it, for there was an excellent government trail all the way, that followed a telegraph line from Shwegun to Papun. Telling Mrs. Hare not to be afraid, we crossed the river in a sampan, and set off. The moon was nearly full, the trail was easy, and hour by hour we walked the miles away during that close tropical evening. About midnight, when we had covered nearly half the distance, the moonlight suddenly disappeared, and, looking up, we saw to our sorrow that the sky was overcast with the heaviest, blackest thunderclouds imaginable.

"It's going to rain, Thara," I said.

"And we're going to get wet," he replied.

And the next minute the battle of the elements started in fearful tropical fashion. The thunder roared till the jungle vibrated. The lightning cracked and crackled till we were blinded with its fury, and it rained. It rained as only a Burma thunderstorm can rain.

"Where's the nearest village, Thara?" I asked.

"Behind us," he answered, "but we can't go back. If we are going to get through we must keep on going."

We kept on. The trail was full of water in no time, but the lightning revealed quite vividly the galvanized iron telegraph poles a furlong apart, which we followed as best we could. We went a mile or two, then found the water getting deeper and deeper, till it was up to our necks.

"Wait a minute, Thara," I shouted. "Let's see where we are."

The next flash of lightning revealed four tall posts just in front of us, with a wire ladder going up to them. What a relief!

"It's just a creek, Thara," I called, "and here's a hanging wire bridge for us to cross over."

We half swam, half tiptoed, to the ladder and crawled up, and sure enough there was the bridge about three feet wide with wooden slats securely wired on, sagging away down, across, and up to a corresponding tower on the other side.

"I wonder if the sag is still above water?" Tha Myaing mused half to himself.

"I'll soon tell you," I replied, and on our hands and knees, hanging on for dear life, we started across. Down—down—down. Suddenly there was a blinding flash, followed by a roar and an explosion as a thunderbolt hit a tree about two hundred feet away. The air around us was so charged with static electricity that we were temporarily benumbed, and for a moment we just hung on in silence.

"Are you all right, Thara?" I finally ventured.

134

"Yes, but I feel funny all over, and I can't move," Tha Myaing replied.

"Then hang on for dear life," I called.

"I'm better now. Let's move," he answered, and we continued to crawl cautiously forward. Soon we realized that we were ascending the opposite incline, and we knew that the sag was above water. Up—up—up to the tower, down the ladder into water not quite so deep as on the opposite bank, then forward we went.

"Any more bridges like this, Thara?" I asked.

"Two more, I think," he replied as cheerfully as he could, but we had soon passed them without any difficulty, and a mile or two more brought us to the end of the jungle and onto the edge of the three-mile-wide Mezita rice fields. On reaching the rice fields, we gave a shout, but as we stood looking for directions, revealed in the lightning flashes, we shuddered, for the rice field was filled with water. It had become a sea, and though we could pick out the telegraph poles still poking up above the water as far as we could see, we wondered ruefully how deep the water was.

On we plunged. We could see much better in the open, but progress was slow as we stumbled over and through the terraced rice fields. Though some were shallow and some were deep, we noticed that they were all getting deeper as we proceeded, and we were soon up to our waists.

"Are we half way across yet, Thara?" I asked.

"Almost. Let's keep going," Tha Myaing replied. "It looks as though the devils are angry with us tonight, doesn't it?"

Having no intention or desire to stop just then, I just mumbled, "Yes," and kept going, but I must confess that the distance and the storm were telling on my strength, and I was getting tired. Deeper—deeper—deeper it got as we stumbled on. Up to our armpits! Up to our necks!

"Wait a minute, Thara! Let us see where we are," I shouted. "It's getting deeper."

But there was no response from Tha Myaung.

"Oh, Thara!" I yelled again with all my strength. A flash of lightning enabled me to look around, but Tha Myaung was not there. He had disappeared.

Buried Treasure

"And they shall be Mine, saith the Lord of hosts, in that day when I make up My jewels." Malachi 3:17.

God Had Heard Ba Twe's Prayer and Helped Him Find the Buffaloes,
Even Though He Was a Heathen

CHAPTER 7

Buried Treasure

>+>+>+>+>+>+>+>+>+

FOR A MOMENT I was overwhelmed with panic.
Then once more I yelled, "Oh—Thara. Oh—Thara," and
like sweetest music to my ears I heard him shout a long
way off, "Here I am. Here I am."

"Where?" I asked.

"Down here!" he answered. "It's just the irrigating ditch
in the middle of the paddy field, Thara. It isn't so deep
over here. Come on across."

"But where's the bridge?"

"There isn't any."

"Then how can I get across?"

"Do as I did, Thara," he encouraged. "Just fall in and
swim, and soon you'll be here."

There was no disguising the fact that I had to do
something, and, as this was about the only thing there
was to do, I plunged in and swam in the direction of his
voice, and before long I was with Tha Myaing again.

We looked for our telegraph poles, took our direction,

and plodded on. The water was getting more and more shallow every terrace we came to. It was down to our waists again. Surely there could be only about one more mile of this, but the mud was heavy, and my strength was gone. We spoke very little. I can only remember an overwhelming desire to sit down and rest in mud and water that would submerge me to my neck again, when right then the storm above us gathered itself for one more mighty final outburst. The thunder roared and pealed about our very heads. The lightning in terrifying cracks dazzled our eyes with its blinding brilliance. I shut my eyes and shuddered with fear. At that moment, when my courage was at its lowest ebb, when my strength was gone, while I had closed my eyes to the terror of the lightning, Tha Myaing, with his face resolutely turned homeward and his eyes shaded with his uplifted hands, saw clearly and distinctly the silhouette of the palm trees at the edge of the paddy field lake—the palm trees that were very close to our mission station, and he shouted, "Look, Thara! Look! We are nearly home!"

What marvelous strength and courage there were in those words.

"Nearly home?" I shaded my eyes and looked. There, sure enough, were the palms just ahead. We *were* nearly home. I gathered every ounce of strength that I had left, and on we went. What a wonderful thought! What a wonderful sermon! When the storm was at its worst, and fear threatened to make my heart fail, we were nearly home! Sustained by this blessed assurance, we pressed on. The rain soon stopped, and we reached home at four in the morning. We changed our clothes, had a bite to eat and a hot drink, then jumped into the motor launch and chugged down the river to Shwegun to get Mrs. Hare, the children, and the forty-four boxes and bundles that were on the ship.

"I don't see how you possibly got through that awful storm last night," said Mrs. Hare as we started off safe and sound in the mission launch, with nothing more to fear.

"If the devils had had their way, my dear," I said, "we never could have done it, but our God was able to deliver us, for He is the living God and steadfast forever. He delivereth and rescueth, and He worketh signs and wonders in heaven and in earth."

That is why I love to magnify His name and His power. That is why I never tire to tell of the treasure that His right arm has won. That is why I delight to tell how in His own mysterious ways He has dug, quarried out, and cut His precious jewels from the land of the haunted pagoda, then polished and polished till His likeness is seen in them.

How well I remember one year when we were opening school and I was registering the students, that a tall awkward-looking lad stood beside me.

"What's your name, my boy?" I asked.

"Ba Twe," he replied.

"How old are you?"

"Twelve summers."

"And what's your religion?" I continued.

"My what?"

"Your *religion*," I emphasized.

"What's that?" he again asked blankly.

"Why," I said, "that means what you worship. Do you worship the pagodas and the Buddhist priests?"

"Oh, yes! yes!" And I was just about to write down a capital B beside his name for Buddhist, when he added quickly, "But, Thara, I hardly think you could call us

141

Buddhist, for we do not worship the pagodas and priests often enough for that. Not every full moon.

"Then are you a spirit worshiper?"

"Yes, yes." He smiled.

"And you have the altar where you put the flowers and the rice for the devils?"

"Yes, yes," he continued, and I was just about to write down a capital A for Animist, for that is what we call the devil worshipers, when he interrupted. "But—but we are not very good spirit worshipers, Thara. We do not always make the sacrifices as we should. No, I think you shouldn't call us Animists."

"Then," I queried, "what shall I call you? Are you a Christian?"

"Oh, no! no!" And after a moment of puzzled thought he added, "I think you'd better just call me plain heathen."

I accordingly wrote down "heathen" and Ba Twe came to school.

Little did the lad realize what a tremendous change our school would make in him. He gave up his swearing, drinking, and smoking so easily that it seemed he had always lived free from these vices. He washed his clothes and combed his hair, and enjoyed it so much that it seemed he had always been clean. He came to Sabbath school and enjoyed it, but would never take part.

"Oh, no," he would say. "I'm a heathen. God would not like me to do anything."

He came to prayer meeting and to Friday night testimony meeting, but he would never take part.

"Oh, no," he would explain, "I'm a heathen. God would not listen to my prayer or talk." So all through the year he went about thinking he really was a heathen.

142

When the summer vacation came, he went back to his village at the foot of the mountains. There he saw the real heathen village boys cursing, smoking, drinking, unwashed and filthy, and instinctively he shrank from them. "Ugh," he shuddered. "I thought I was a heathen, but I surely am not like one of them. Now I'm not a Buddhist, I'm not a spirit worshiper, I'm not a Christian, and I'm not a heathen. So what am I?"

Since no one could read his thoughts, nobody offered him any help on this mighty problem, and for a time Ba Twe didn't know just exactly what he was. Then one day something happened that made it all clear. He had been minding his father's two buffaloes in the jungle, a boy's ideal of a job, for he sat on the back of one buffalo and drove the other along with little clay marbles propelled from a bamboo bow, so that before long they had eaten their fill of the luscious green grass at the roadside, and contentedly lay down in the shade of some friendly trees to chew the cud. Having nothing else to do, Ba Twe lay down beside them and was soon fast asleep.

"If the buffaloes wander away, I am sure to know it. If they stir, I am sure to waken," he thought. But the buffaloes stirred and wandered away while he slept on and on. When at last he awakened with a start, the sun was setting. He rubbed his eyes and suddenly remembered his buffaloes. They were gone.

"Oh, what shall I do?" he groaned. "Father will be so angry. They have strayed away into someone's garden. There will be a fine and oh, what trouble I'll be in."

Quickly he jumped up and frantically raced up and down yelling and shouting, hoping to find his buffaloes. But no friendly moo answered him. Down to the riverbank, up

143

to the rice fields he went, but not a sight or sound of his buffaloes anywhere.

"Oh, what will I do?" he groaned. "What will I do?" Just then he came to an old dead tree. "I'll climb up to the top of this," he said, "and use it for a tower." In a few minutes he was at the top of the tree and could see all around the valley. There were buffaloes everywhere, plenty of them, but they had boys on their backs driving them home. Sick with anxiety, he concluded that his buffaloes were really lost.

"Oh, what will I do?" he groaned aloud, and right there in the top of the old dead tree, a little voice spoke to his heart and said, "Pray! Pray!"

"Oh, no!" he argued with it. "God would not like to hear me pray. I'm a heath——but no, I'm not. I'm not a heathen." He thought a moment, and, "But I'm not a Christian anyway. I couldn't. I couldn't."

But the little voice kept on saying in his heart, "Pray! Pray! Pray!"

Now, there was not another thing he could do, so, shutting his eyes and hanging onto the top of the old dead tree for all he was worth, he prayed, "O God, help me find my buffaloes."

He should have said, "for Jesus' sake, Amen," but he could not. He was too frightened. He had been talking to the living God, and he rather expected that God would smite him with a flash of lightning. In sudden fear he started off down the old dead tree with his heart pounding—down, down, limb by limb. The last branch being ten feet from the ground, he made it in a single jump, and landed in the soft green grass—kerplunk! And even as he did—Moo-oo! sounded right behind him, and there were his buffaloes.

"Well, well!" gasped Ba Twe. "He did! He did hear me!" He stood amazed for a moment, then mounting one buffalo he began to drive the other home, and while he was driving his buffaloes home, *it happened*—the conviction gripped him that he now knew what his religion was. He was a God worshiper—a Christian.

I remember the first Friday night after school had opened the following year. Ba Twe was there, and while the students were telling of their vacation experiences, he too rose and when his turn came he told the story I have just recorded. Then turning to his fellow students, he said, "If God would listen to my little prayer before I was a proper Christian, then I have decided to give my life to Him and to serve Him forever."

Ba Twe stayed at school till he had finished the seventh grade, which was as far as that school went, and proved himself to be a true, faithful Christian. He dreamed of going to the advanced school at Meiktila, but in 1934 the hardest year of depression hit our jungle. The price of rice fell from one rupee, eight annas (50c) a bushel to eight annas (16c) a bushel, and it was all the jungle people could do to buy oil and salt to eat with their rice, much less clothes and books and railroad tickets for an education. The mission funds were all cut, and it was impossible to put any new village teachers into the field. It was a very serious lad who went back to his father's farm after graduation.

For the longest time he sat on the bamboo floor, wrapped in thought, then suddenly looking up at his father, he said, "Dad, do you need me on the farm this year?"

"Oh, no, my son. I think I can manage. You can go to school again all right."

"But, Father, that is the trouble. I have finished all

the studies at the Ohn Daw school, and even if I could buy my railroad ticket to Meiktila I could get no work. No, I cannot go to school."

"Then where will you go, my son?"

"Oh, Father, listen. I will tell you what is in my heart. I have given my life to Jesus. I have promised to serve Him forever. The mission cannot give me work. I cannot go to school. You do not need me on the farm. So I would go to those who speak our language on the hills of Siam, where there is no teacher, and I would serve the Master there."

"But—my son——"

"Never mind the money, Father. The village folks will call me to eat with them, and I will carry some medicines for the sick ones and some Memory Verse Cards for the children. Father, I must go."

For a moment the father thought, and then simply replied, "Go—go, my son, and God go with you."

Three weeks later a vacancy occurred in Rangoon. A caretaker was needed for our mission property there. They remembered faithful Ba Twe, and telegraphed Pastor Peter to inform him of his appointment. With all speed Peter took the river steamer, and, arriving at the little farm at the foot of the hills, inquired, "Where is Ba Twe?"

"Gone to Siam," said the father, pointing eastward toward the boundary hills.

"Siam?" said Peter in surprise.

"Yes, gone to Siam to be a self-supporting preacher."

"He has? and here I have a job for him at thirty rupees a month."

"Thirty rupees a month!" His older brother suddenly came to life. That seemed like a fortune to him. What could they not do if one of the family was earning thirty rupees a month! It was a gold mine! "Say," he said, "I think— maybe—I know just about where he has gone. I need to cut bamboos anyway. Hold the job open for him ten days, and I think I can find him."

They held the job open for ten days, but the big brother came back alone. "I cannot catch up with him," he explained. "Everywhere I go he has been there, giving medicines to the sick ones, showing pictures, and telling stories from the Golden Book to the children who eagerly press around him. But he is always ahead of me, and I cannot catch up with him."

"When his medicines run out, he'll come back for some more," added the father "then we can tell him."

They waited a month, but Ba Twe did not come back —two months, three, four, five, six months, but Ba Twe never came back.

Then one day into our jungle dispensary there came a little old lady from the hills. "I want some medicine like the missionary had for sick babies," she said.

"Where do you live?" asked Yeh Ni, the nurse.

"In Siam," the old lady replied.

"Away over in Siam!" said Yeh Ni incredulously.

"Yes," nodded the old lady, "it has taken me five days to get here."

"But how did you know there was a hospital here?"

"Why, your missionary told us."

"Our missionary? Why, Auntie, we have no missionary over there."

"Oh, yes, you did have. You did have," she said, "a big tall boy with a big bag on his shoulder, and he treated the sick with his medicines and told the children lovely stories from the Golden Book. Oh, how we all loved him. You had a missionary over there all right, and he always told us, before he died, to come and get medicines here."

Yeh Ni, the nurse, started. As the old lady had described our missionary on the Siam hills, suddenly she had recognized Ba Twe, the Missionary Volunteer.

"He's dead, you said? Ba Twe's dead?"

"Oh, yes. I forgot to tell you. Three weeks ago he got malignant malaria fever. There was no medicine left; he had used it all on others. There was nothing we could do, so he died, and we buried him on the side of the hill overlooking our village."

That night it was as though a black-out settled down over the Ohn Daw Mission Station. "Ba Twe's dead," they whispered to each other. "Ba Twe—is dead," and tears flowed silently for the hero who had given his life for Siam.

The next Sabbath afternoon, as leader of the young peoples' meeting, Yeh Ni, the nurse, told a story—a story of buried treasure—treasure more precious than gold or silver—buried in the lonely hills of Siam. Then she said, her voice breaking in choked sobs, "Now we are going to take another collection, and we are going to keep on taking more collections until someday we can have another missionary in Ba Twe's place." And our Karen young people set their faces toward Siam, as the Chinese young people have set their faces toward Tibet, and they prayed for and talked about Siam as they never had before.

Then came a day about two years later when a call came from Siam. "We have money to support a new family for the Karens on our borderland," they said. "Is there not a young Karen man in Burma with college education who would volunteer for this difficult field?"

The superintendent folded the letter and began to feel for words with which to make his appeal, but the appeal was not needed.

"I'll go," said Kale Paw, springing to his feet. He had just graduated from our South India College.

"But, Kale Paw," said the superintendent, "you could not go! Why, Kale Paw, we have a place all ready for you on the faculty of our training school at Meiktila. No, no, we couldn't send you Kale Paw, and anyway you are not married yet, and that post on the hills will be the most lonely——"

He stopped, for suddenly all eyes had turned toward Yeh Ni, the nurse, who sat there quietly blushing, and all were smiling as though they had heard a little more than the superintendent had about Kale Paw's having to remain single very long, and it took him but a moment to conclude that Kale Paw and Yeh Ni had talked it all over and decided to volunteer their services—bless their hearts.

The arrangements were accordingly made, and they sent Yeh Ni and Kale Paw to the lonely hills of Siam, to the land of our buried treasure, and the light that was lit by Ba Twe, the lone Missionary Volunteer, was kept shining. The banner of the third angel's message was kept waving triumphantly.

But at last there came a day when we had to say good-by. It became necessary, after nearly twenty years of service, to return to the homeland for a season to educate our children. Of course, Eileen and Lenny would benefit greatly from the privileges of academy and college training, but the one who would mostly benefit was our little five-year-old Verna May, who had become deaf following a very severe illness when she was ten months old. Education in an oral school at home seeming to be imperative for her, a transfer was made, and with heavy hearts we got ready to leave. Our furniture was sold, our boxes packed, our farewells said. At four o'clock in the morning, while Peter and San Yok brought the motor launch to the landing, we bowed in our bungalow to pray that God would protect us while we traveled, and take us safely all the way. Then, opening the back door, we slipped out into the darkness, for the day had not yet dawned.

As we did so we were startled with the strange sound of about three hundred people striking three hundred matches as they lit three hundred candles. What a sight! Commencing at the foot of the stairs, we saw the winding stream of light reach right down to the launch landing and realized that more than three hundred people were there to say good-by to the missionaries they had learned to love. For just a second I remembered how they had run from us screaming, *"Dawtaka! Dawtaka!"* just twenty years before. We began to shake hands, slowly going down the line. There were the teachers, their wives and their children. How well we knew them all! How hard it was to part! We were nearly beyond words when an old lady grasped my hand and said, "Thara, I'm Clever Queen's grandma, and I'm still a heathen, but I did want to come and shake hands good-by. We're not afraid of you any more now, and we want you to come back, and, Thara," she added, "you've been happy up here too, haven't you?"

"Yes, Grandma," I said.

"And when you first came here you were very thin, and now you're very fat, aren't you?" she went on.

"Yes, Grandma," I replied.

"And when you first came to live here you didn't have

any children, and now you have four, haven't you?"

"Yes, Grandma," I said.

"Do you know why?" she asked confidentially.

"I think I do, Grandma, but what do you think has made us happy here?"

"We don't think. We *know*," she declared positively. "It's because—It's because you haven't been fooling with the treasure from the haunted pagoda."

"Now, now, Grandma," I said. "You surely don't believe that that treasure is still there."

"Of course it is! Of course it is!" she said rather surprised that I could have any doubt as to what she knew. "And there's them that says how a white man—a miner— came up here once before you did, and he found the treasure, a canoe two-thirds full of silver bricks, but as soon as he touched it he began to itch. And he itched and itched, and he scratched and scratched all the way down to Moulmein, and all the medicine he got didn't do it any good. He still itched and he still scratched. At last he went to a Burmese doctor, and the doctor took one look and said, 'You've got haunted treasure itch, and it won't get better till you put the treasure back,' but the man didn't want to, so he itched and he scratched, till at last he couldn't sleep for itching and he couldn't eat for scratching. Then he said, 'Treasure or no treasure, I'll die if I keep scratching.' And he brought it back and put it in the hole again and covered it up; and do you know? When he put the last shovelful of dirt on top of it, he stopped itching. So there now!"

"But, Grandma," I said, also confidentially, "don't you know? Haven't you heard? Didn't anyone ever tell you? We *have* got the treasure."

151

"You have?" she gasped.

"Yes," I assured her.

"Was it silver bricks?"

"Oh, Grandma, better than that," I said. "Rubies and diamonds, silver and brass and gold."

"You did! and to think I never ———"

"Would you like to see it?" I asked in a whisper.

"Oh, yes, Thara," she answered, trembling with excitement.

"Here it is," I said, pointing to the boys and girls and the men and women who had been won from the darkness of superstition to the light of God's love. "Look, there's Ohn Bwint and Tay Po. There's Father Knife and Galvanized Iron. There's Mg Thein and Very Tall. There's Clever Queen and Clear Gold. There's Hla Kin and Naw Kya Tee. There's See See and Barnabus, and all our other jungle heroes, and they are all more precious than gold."

"Oh, that kind of treasure!" she exclaimed as she grasped what I was saying.

"And, Grandma, God wants you to be part of His treasure too."

As we talked, the band began to play "God Be With You Till We Meet Again," and the company tried to join in with them, but their hearts were too heavy for song, and my voice was too choked for words as I added.

"Listen to it, Grandma! That's real treasure. That's the treasure that was worth digging."

And as I moved off down the line, still shaking hands good-by, I could hear the old lady saying, "I believe you're right! I believe you're right!"

We came home to America in 1934, and for six years Thara Peter and his associates carried on the work up and down the Salween River, while Verna May made rapid progress in her lip-reading school and Eileen and Lenny enjoyed their academy and college education. Then one day we were ready to go back to Burma.

Eileen had found some treasure of her own while in Pacific Union College, and with her husband had gone to India in 1940, so we said good-by to Lenny, told him to get ready quickly to come and join us. Then, gathering up some more brass horns for the jungle band, in June, 1941, we set sail again for the land of the haunted pagoda. We were going back to dig for more treasure.

But the powers of darkness were ill content to let their slaves be freed. This kind of treasure digging was going on all through the Orient, and evil spirits decided to do something about it. They breathed hate for the white man into the hearts of the children of the East, and poured contempt on the religion he had brought. We arrived in Burma just two months before Japan turned in devouring fury to try to drive the white man out and burn up with persecution the treasure he had won—just two months before Pearl Harbor.

8

The Furnace of Affliction

✕✕✕✕✕✕✕✕✕✕

"I have refined thee, but not with silver; I have chosen thee in the furnace of affliction." Isaiah 48:10.

We Took Our Place in the Fleeing Procession of Homeless Evacuees From Rangoon

CHAPTER 8

The Furnace of Affliction

>+>+>+>+>+>+>+>+>+

T HE SUN ROSE in Rangoon on the morning of December 7, 1941, and gilded the Shwe Dagon Pagoda just as it had risen any other day before. Heralded by the cawing of thousands of crows and the tinkling of tiny temple bells, it seemingly introduced just another peaceful, balmy, tropical day; and Rangoon's 400,000 rose up to eat and to drink, to buy and to sell, to plant and to build, to marry and to be given in marriage. But ere the sun had set that evening, tidings from the East had brought trouble to every heart, for it was on that fateful day that Japan had declared war against England and America, and had struck viciously at Pearl Harbor, Hong Kong, and Manila. The seventh day after war was declared enemy planes were flying overhead.

Fortunately no bombs were dropped that day, but an indescribable fear seized upon thousands and thousands of the inhabitants of the city, and the evacuation of the city commenced immediately. The trains and river boats were crowded, and for miles and miles, along every road, hundreds and hundreds of people, walking, riding in gharries and rickshas, pushing handcarts, loaded with their few worldly possessions, were fleeing in terror from the city.

The next day, however, was quiet. No airplanes came, no siren sounded. And, though a mysterious woman's voice from Tokyo kept warning the Burmese people to get out of the city, for two days nothing happened. Three—four days. Not knowing what might happen, and being anxious to be found at my post of duty whatever might happen, I hastened off up the Salween River to Kamamaung, my dear old mission station, to spend a week of special meetings with my jungle treasure. Five—six—seven days went by. The evacuation of Rangoon ceased; some began to return. Eight —nine—ten days, and then it came! It came unexpectedly, while men were boasting of safety. Peter, the Karen mission superintendent, and I were coming down the Salween River on December 23, when suddenly, near the halfway town of Paan, we heard a mighty roar overhead, and looking up, we saw fifteen enemy planes in one group and twenty-seven in another headed straight for Rangoon.

"There they go," whispered Peter.

I didn't answer. No answer was needed. My heart was shocked to a strange numbness as I realized that they were headed straight to the city where my home was and where my wife and children were. How glad I was to find Mrs. Hare and the children safe and our home still standing when I arrived the next morning, but what a story they had to tell.

As the siren wailed its warning, they had scrambled into a big cement gutter about four feet deep and two feet

158

wide, running at the back of our house. At ten-thirty, straight from the East, riding on the beams of the rising sun, came fifty-one enemy planes. And soon, seemingly right overhead, they saw the "yellow bellies," as everyone called them, dropping their "eggs." The next instant they saw our "flying tigers" giving them battle in their P-40's. They saw the machine-gunning. They saw the great clouds of smoke. They saw the leaping tongues of fire and heard the screaming, the crying, the yelling, the shouting, of the thousands who were fleeing from the destruction. They saw three enemy planes shot out of the air. They saw the Japanese pilots bale out in their parachutes. One chute failed to open, and we learned afterward that that pilot dropped right into the cemetery. Two others, landing in the city and finding themselves surrounded by policemen and about to be arrested, committed hara-kiri; that is, they ripped open their abdomens and bled to death. As another came floating down, he began machine-gunning the women and children who were looking on. One of our pillboxes near by replied in the same language and literally sawed off his dangling legs in mid-air and tore his chute to ribbons so that his legless body fell to its death on the pavement below.

Rangoon had been told to go to the trenches when the siren blew, but the dogfight in the air was too fascinating. Instead of taking cover as they should, thousands upon thousands stood in the streets looking on, with the result that thirteen hundred and fifty met sudden death in the destruction that rained from the skies that day, and twice that number were taken to the city's hospitals. All the rest of that day and all the next were spent by the city municipal department and volunteer groups repairing broken water

159

mains, filling up the bomb craters in the main thorough-
fares, cleaning up the debris, and disposing of the dead,
while every hour some more gruesome and tragic discovery
was made. Perhaps the saddest of all was where a bomb had
broken through the roof and burst in a room in which a
mother and her three little children were crouching for
safety. The mangled form of the unborn babe was found
on the window sill, and arms and legs and heads and por-
tions of bodies were scattered all over the brick ruins. The
volunteer group that found them tried to put the bodies
together again to give them a proper burial, but it couldn't
be done, and they had to be satisfied with burying the remains all together in one common bag outside the city.

Well we knew why Japan was striking at Rangoon, for
you remember Rangoon is not only the capital of Burma
but also the beginning of the famous Burma Road, the
vital life line to poor China. From Rangoon a good motor
road and a railway led to Lashio, six hundred and twenty
miles away, and from there seven hundred more hilly,
crooked miles led across the border to Kunming. In the city's
factories thirty thousand trucks were in the process of being
assembled. Every day from two hundred to three hundred
were rolled off the assembly lines, loaded with war materials
and ammunition, and sent off into China.

We realized that Japan would strike again and again in
an attempt to close this door to China, and we didn't have
long to wait for the next raid, for on Christmas Day the
planes returned. They came about ten-forty-five, just as our
little ones were wondering if we could eat Christmas dinner
at home that day or whether we would have to grab it and
eat it in the gutter, as they had the day before. But when
the siren screams, there is no time to think of Christmas

dinners. There's only one thing to do, and that is to go to the trenches. So down we went all together. From our cement gutter we watched our planes roar off to intercept the invaders. They met seventy-five enemy planes ten miles away, and during the next half hour shot down twenty-one of them into the paddy fields outside the city, but four yellow-bellies finally slipped through our formations and dropped one hundred and eleven incendiary bombs over another section of the city. Again we heard the awful explosions. Again we saw the great clouds of smoke. Again we heard the crackle of flames and the panicky cries of the fleeing thousands.

One of our major mission projects at this time in Rangoon was the loading of sixteen huge trucks with medical and mission supplies for our inland China missions. Mr. Coberly, who was in charge of this project, placed one of these trucks at our disposal. With Dr. Walker, from our city clinic, we organized an improvised ambulance unit and on Christmas Day, as soon as the explosions were over, we rushed off to see what we could do. I cannot describe our feelings when we saw magnificent buildings like the state mental hospital and the Cushing High School, as well as scores of magnificent homes and hundreds of poorer homes, all blasted to ruins and going up in flames. We were directed by the air-raid warden to a section near the car barns, and in about two and one-half hours, from among ruined buildings, we took seventeen who were still living to the hospital. I don't want to write of the mutilation we saw. I'm trying to forget that, but the shudder caused by the first time I stumbled over a human head rolling in the dust and by the first time I picked up a severed leg will haunt me forever.

11   161

As Mr. Coberly's convoy might leave any moment, we realized that we couldn't serve best as an independent ambulance unit, so with others I very soon joined the civil defense workers as a St. John's ambulance driver, and it was my privilege and pleasure to serve in this capacity until the last day of Rangoon's freedom, when all foreign civilians were evacuated.

After Christmas the planes came almost every day. They came by day; they came by night; some of the dog-fights we witnessed were thrilling, but the irregularity of it and the uncertainty of it all, together with the hours we were forced to be cramped up in the trenches, became very nerve wearing.

Early in January the invasion of Burma began at two points: in the South near Tavoy, and on the southeast border about eighty miles from Moulmein.

The American consul at once began to urge us to get our women and children out to India. "You know," he said, "we all hope for the best, but I am afraid that we are in for a dirty time here in Rangoon, and we will feel much happier if we know our women and children are safe and sound in Calcutta."

Seeing wisdom in the consul's advice, we went to the shipping offices to book passages for our twelve women and fifteen children, and I wish you could have heard the agents' reply.

"Well, you know we haven't had any kind of ship for two weeks," they said, "and goodness only knows if ever there will be another one. But we don't mind adding your names to the waiting list. We have three thousand names on it already, and it won't hurt to add a few more," and we went out of that office without any human hope that they would ever get to India. It almost looked as if the wrath of the evil one would swallow us up, but we were sustained by the promise that God would be as a little sanctuary to us in this foreign country, and that, if it pleased Him, He could open up a way of escape and take them across. The only thing we could do was to get them ready and wait.

January 20 the telephone rang and the consul unexpectedly announced, "We have a little freighter going to Calcutta. It has just unloaded some tanks and bombs. It's not listed with the steamship agents, but if you can get some of your women and children to the wharf by 3 P.M., we'll take them across for you."

It gave us just one and a half hours to bundle up their bedding and pack their suitcases, but by 3 P.M., with the help of Mr. Coberly and one of his China trucks, the first group of our evacuee women and children got safely away with a group of other missionaries, some of whom had fled overland from Bangkok. Two days later we were staggered with the news that a boat had been torpedoed and sunk by enemy submarines on its way to Rangoon from Calcutta. In two more days another boat was sunk, the passengers and crew coming ashore on the southern coast of Burma in lifeboats and on rafts. There were some who said, "How does it feel to know that your wives and children too are at the bottom of the deep, blue sea?" But we said, "We don't know it, and until we do we are going to believe that God has taken them safely across."

And you can't begin to imagine how thrilled we were when almost a week later we received an air-mail letter from Mrs. Hare, in which she said, "As our little freighter sailed out of the Rangoon River into the Bay of Bengal, a thick, heavy fog settled down around us, and we couldn't see the

163

sun for four days. Not until we were in the Hooghly River, on our way up to Calcutta, did the sun shine again. Then, when we landed and bought the first newspaper, we read that two boats had been torpedoed and sunk while we were *covered with the cloud.*" The white man's God was still stronger than the devils.

A week later another little freighter took some more of our women and children across. By February 3, the last of our foreign women and children were taken safely across to Calcutta. For three weeks the Japanese hordes had been advancing. The old port of Moulmein, on the Salween River, had fallen, so that we felt like celebrating when Mr. Coberly got back with his truck that afternoon. We shook his hand and expressed our appreciation for all he had done, but to our surprise, he said, "Good-by, gentlemen!"

"Now, come, Coberly," I said, "we're just beginning to like you, and you're going off to leave us now?"

And he replied, "Gentlemen, it's *strange,* to say the least, but you know my sixteen trucks have been practically all loaded for six weeks. I've just been waiting for my final clearance papers from the customs house. Every day I go around. Every day they shake their heads and say, 'Not finished yet, Mr. Coberly, not finished yet. Come tomorrow.' Now, almost from habit I called in at the customs office on my way home from the wharf after taking the *last* of your women and children to the boat, and as I entered the door, the clerk smiled and said, 'All finished, Mr. Coberly. All finished. Here you are. You can leave any time.' So now we're all ready to go. We'll be starting off as the moon comes up tonight, God willing and siren permitting."

I took my hat off and stood at attention for a moment in honor of this brave group of men and women who, in spite of the terrors of war, in spite of the fact that Rangoon was crumbling around them, were turning their faces toward the vast, remote, lonely, interior of China. In Kalaw, our hill station, we had five young missionary families who had just completed a year of studying the Chinese language. Those young men had flown their wives in to Chungking by plane, and each one was now ready to take the wheel of one of those trucks and drive it over the Burma Road.

Fain would I have waited till the convoy left at 10 P.M. to wave good-by to these brave men. Fain would I have waited to breathe a little prayer that God would protect them on their perilous journey, but as this was one of my many nights on ambulance duty, I walked into the center of the city with my tin hat slung on my shoulder and signed in for duty in the basement of the great City Hall. It was an interesting evening. There were five men on all-night duty, a bank manager, two motor house managers, a university professor, and myself. We were given our ambulance numbers and keys, and immediately checked the ambulances over for petrol, stretchers, bandages, and splints. Then we went to an adjoining room, where sixty native boys were drilled as litter bearers, called the roll on the group that had been assigned to us, then, satisfied that we were ready for any emergency, we sat down to talk about the news and rumors of the day. At 9:30 P.M. we tuned in to the news broadcast from London, and I was sitting in front of the radio, listening intently to every word as it came through the air, when something attracted by eyes just outside the windows. I looked to see. The great shutters were folded back against the concrete walls of the City Hall, and there, rising above the irregular city horizon, was the ten-o'clock moon. I thought of Coberly and his brave

165

companions. I thought of their sixteen trucks all ready to leave. I wanted to go outside where I could be alone with my thoughts. I rose and moved toward the door, but before I reached it the telephone rang.

I stopped and watched the night clerk pick up the receiver—and immediately he called, "Alert!"

"Alert! Alert!" echoed the first-aid sergeants, and sixty men ran to positions. Shutters were closed and lights extinguished, and we sat down in the darkness, feeling for our blankets. By this time the siren was screaming its warning to the public. It was the sixtieth air raid to come to Rangoon. The people now knew what to do and how to do it, and, without any sign of panic, with their pillows and rugs under their arms, they came swarming into the great bomb-proof shelters in the basement of the City Hall. Hardly had the crowd settled down to quietness before the antiaircraft guns on the river front opened up, and such a bombardment we hadn't heard for many nights. In between the staccato bombardment of the guns, we could hear and feel the deeper boom of the bombs that burst so near that the very cement floor on which we stood vibrated.

"Feels close tonight," said our chief.

"Yes," we whispered.

"I'm afraid we're in for a dirty night," he said.

"We're ready for anything," was our breathed reply, and just then from the doorway came the cry, "Fire! Fire!" and hurrying toward the main doorway, we could see the lurid flames and horrid clouds of black smoke that told us the suburb of Pazundaung, just two miles away, had been hit and was on fire. We heard the fire brigade rattle off through the empty moonlit streets, for the fire brigade is the only vehicle allowed on the streets till "all clear" sounds. But hardly had the fire brigade disappeared into the silence of the distance before the telephone rang again. We held our breath and could hear a police sergeant shouting over the wire, "Five wounded with shrapnel at Pazundaung police station."

The chief turned around and ordered, "Number one ambulance proceed to Pazundaung police station with number one first-aid group as soon as all clear sounds!"

Number one grabbed his blankets, called his first aiders, but had hardly left the room when the telephone rang again. Again we held our breath and listened. This time an air-raid warden was shouting, "Twenty-one wounded with shrapnel at Pazundaung bazaar."

And the chief ordered, "All other ambulances with their first-aid groups report to warden at Pazundaung bazaar as soon as all clear sounds."

We grabbed our blankets and flashlights, called our first aiders, manned our ambulances, waited for the all clear to sound, then roared off through the empty streets to the scene of destruction. Oh, what chaos we found there that night! Telephone poles, electric light poles, splintered, broken, and twisted were lying everywhere. Roofs were blown off, windows shattered, doors torn from their hinges and flung in every direction. Dead dogs, dead horses, and dead people were lying here and there, all lit by the ghastly flames of a near-by burning liquor shop. We drove our ambulances to a parking position and then began our work—our gruesome work of checking the dead and aiding the wounded.

"Better look in here," feebly called a native policeman as I walked around a crater eight feet across in the middle of the street. "There's a Chinese man in there still lying on his bed, and he doesn't come out when we call him. Don't know if he's hurt or not."

I stepped over a dead dog, walked around a dead bullock, and guided by the pale blue light of my flashlight, went up a few steps into the room where the Chinese still lay, seemingly asleep, on his bed. I knelt beside him to give a quick, comprehensive glance, then caught my breath and called back to my first aiders who were right at my heels, "Can't do anything here, boys. All the ambulances and all the doctors in the world couldn't do this poor man any good." A jagged piece of shrapnel from the bomb that had burst just outside had come whizzing through the wall like a buzz saw and had cut off the top of his head.

Awestruck, we were still looking at the gruesome sight, when the subdued murmur of fearful voices outside suddenly rose to a panicky crescendo of shouting and yelling. We listened. The siren was sounding its second warning for that night. What an illuminated target the enemy had made! There were our ambulances still brilliantly lit up by the furiously burning liquor shop.

Onlookers scrambled out of sight. We rushed to our ambulances and drove them into the shade of some trees and waited breathlessly, but no bombs fell. We learned later that our Flying Tigers had been waiting upstairs ever since the first raid, and not only did not a single enemy bomber reach the illuminated target that night but not a single enemy bomber returned to its base near Bangkok. In about twenty minutes the all clear sounded, and in a few hours we had checked about thirty dead and had taken our twenty-one wounded to the hospital.

And that's the way we celebrated the day on which the last of our women and children got safely away to India.

The fires of affliction had fallen upon us. Already Peter and his faithful church members were cut off from us. They were right in the path of the enemy as they swarmed over the border of Siam into Burma. We could only think of them and pray that God would keep them, and use these terrible experiences to purify His peculiar treasure.

The bombings now came more and more frequently. The day after Mr. Coberly left, we had two air raids, but the next day we had six, and the following Sabbath we had eight. They started with the rising of the moon at 2:30 in the morning. At 3:15, 4:00, 5:00, and 6:00 the siren had wailed its warning, and we had spent most of that time in the trenches.

I tell you, it's a terrifying experience to spend half the night in the gutters. The siren screams, down you go, and there you sit in the dark, swatting mosquitoes, scratching mosquito bites, counting the yellow-bellies going over your head, and ducking down when the bombs burst. No indeed, it's no joke, but some of the night battles are thrilling spectacles.

Was it the second or third raid this Sabbath morning? Five waves of enemy bombers passed right over our heads so close we could see the silhouette of the pilots against the pale green exhaust of their engines. Just beyond us our anti-aircraft guns literally opened up their arms to receive them, and we could see their long tracer-bullet fingers reaching up in all directions into the night. Soon the bursting bombs lit up the sky like great flashes of sheet lightning, and we heard the yellow-bellies droning away to the north of the great pagoda. Suddenly a faster, harder purr told us that the night fighters were after them.

Ta-ta-ta-ta, spat a fighter, and the tracer bullets sprayed

169

down like a Fourth of July sky rocket. Ta-ta-ta-ta, answered a yellow-belly, but his tracer bullets didn't reach the fighter. In a second he had swerved to the left and had gone for altitude. Then swooping again savagely on the enemy, Ta-ta-ta-ta, spat the fighter, and we heard the clank of metal. Ta-ta-ta-ta, answered the yellow-belly, but we could see he was in trouble. His wing was off. He tipped, he rolled, he caught on fire and, like a crazy comet, zoomed to the ground. There was a mighty explosion, and flames shot skyward, lighting up the scene. It was night, and out of the darkness lusty cheers and mighty applause came from everywhere.

Yet in spite of all the excitement, when I crawled out of the gutter at 6:30 that Sabbath morning, my head felt like a haystack, and I remembered it would soon be time for Sabbath school. "But," I said to myself, "nobody will come to Sabbath school today. How can they! Everybody has been in the gutters since 2:30 this morning, but, of course, I'm going. I wouldn't stay away from Sabbath school for anything." I dressed, walked to the church, and can you believe it? When the superintendent stood up to open the meeting thirty-seven of our 150 members were there, present and on time. During the bombing we called the roll at the beginning of each Sabbath school session, because everybody wanted to know who had been bombed out and who had been evacuated during the week, and that morning, as the superintendent read the names, we were amazed to find that everyone who was absent had been evacuated to Calcutta or Mandalay or Bassein or some other country place.

I'll never forget the song we sang to open Sabbath school that morning. It was "A Shelter in the Time of Storm," and you should have heard us sing it. Every one of us had had narrow escapes, and it's wonderful how different the words of a hymn sound after you have lived them. I wish you could have heard Mr. Ward and his three children singing that song that morning.

Mr. Ward was a piano tuner. He had lost his dear wife two years before, but his twelve-year-old boy, Stanley, helped him keep the home together for the two little girls, aged nine and eight years. One morning as Mr. Ward left for work he said, "If an air raid comes today, Stanley, take your little sisters to the trench, and daddy will come running home as soon as all clear sounds."

At 10:30 the air-raid signal sounded. Calmly Stanley locked the apartment and took his little sisters downstairs, across the street, and into the big covered city storm drain. It was big enough—two feet wide and four feet deep. It was safe enough—covered with thick concrete slabs, but it was an evil-smelling place with spiders, cobwebs, and rats in abundance, and it was dark. Soon the bombers came droning overhead, and when the bombs began to burst, the two little girls began to cry, but Stanley quickly put his arms around them and said, "Girls, don't be frightened. Look! Listen! Listen! This gutter is just like a cave. Hear how my voice echoes! Come, let's sing, girls, let's sing! Then we won't be able to hear the bombs burst."

And there in that evil-smelling gutter they sang:

"Jesus loves me; this I know,
For the Bible tells me so.
Little ones to Him belong;
We are weak, but He is strong."

And as they sang, their voices echoed and echoed, louder and louder, till they were no longer afraid of the bursting bombs.

171

When the all clear sounded, they crawled back on top of the road, but what a terrible sight! One bomb had blown their front steps away. There were dead people lying everywhere. Broken doors, windows, and pieces of roofing were all over the road. For a minute they stood there bewildered with horror. Then a neighbor lady came running along and said, "We mustn't stay here, children. We mustn't stay here. Let's run! Father will find you some way or other!"

They ran for four miles, till they came to a little empty bamboo house, and they went in to rest and wait for their daddy to come and find them.

Mr. Ward came back when the all clear sounded, but couldn't find his children anywhere. He climbed up the broken timbers to his apartment, but they were not there. He went to the gutter and shouted, "Stanley," but they were not there. He looked over the mangled bodies in the street; he looked under the broken doors and pieces of roofing, but they were not there. He came running to the mission house and gasped, "Help me find my children. I can't find them dead or alive since the raid," and we turned out to help him. All that evening we hunted, and about ten o'clock that night Mr. Meleen heard where they were. It was the next day that I saw Stanley, and I said, "Stanley, weren't you scared?"

"No-o-o," he said in real junior style. "Mr. Hare, I'll tell you, when the bombs burst, you sing! Sing! And especially if you are in a smelly gutter your voice will echo and echo till you can't hear the bombs burst." I've been telling everybody ever since to "sing when the bombs are bursting." The Ward children were there at the Sabbath school that morning singing "A Shelter in the Time of Storm." I wish you could have heard them.

Mr. Martin was there with his wife too. He was one of

the customs officials, and one day when he came home for dinner he had just parked his car under the porch when the siren began to wail its warning. Down into the trench at the back of their house he ran with his wife. But hardly had they seated themselves in the dugout when a direct hit blew their home to smithereens. His car caught on fire and burned to ashes, But he was not even scratched, nor was his wife. And they were at Sabbath school that morning singing, "A Shelter in the Time of Storm." I wish you could have heard them too.

Mr. Ross was also with us. He was an electrician. He was baptized the day that we had our first air raid. One day he was at the top of a pole repairing some wires when the siren sounded, but he couldn't hear it for the confusion in the street below. Suddenly the bombs began to burst. He shouted to his five assistants to run to the shelters, while he unbuckled his belt, sprang down the ladder, and threw himself face down into the shallow curbside gutter. Just as he pulled one of his men down beside him a bomb burst near by. He felt the pavement heave. The shrapnel flew above him, demolishing doors, windows, trees, and vehicles, and mowing down the people in the streets. Four of his assistants were killed instantly, but he wasn't even scratched. I wish you could have heard him sing "A Shelter in the Time of Storm."

Oh, it is true! the fires of trouble and affliction do make the treasure shine brighter!

For nearly two weeks our troops held the Japanese forces at Moulmein. The Salween River made a natural barrier, and our hopes were running high. But the traitorous Burmese dressed the Japanese soldiers up as women and country farmers, smuggled them across the river in canoes

173

and river boats, led them by unseen foot trails and tidal creeks till enough of them had infiltrated to endanger our forward flank, and on February 11 we were startled to read that the enemy had crossed the Salween and our forces had taken up new positions at Thaton. Then we knew the fate of Rangoon was sealed. It was only a matter of time, maybe only days, before it too would fall, for there were no more great natural barriers.

We men who still remained now gave ourselves in earnest to evacuating all of our church members. We took them to the trains and the river boats, and in between we sat down to pack our one suitcase, for our only way of escape was by Pastor Christensen's car, and if four men could get one suitcase each and a bundle of rugs in addition to the gasoline necessary for the journey northward, it was all we could expect.

What an ordeal! If sudden destruction snatched from you every worldly possession, I think it would be easier to say "Thy will be done" and praise God for preserving your life than to sit down and coolly choose from your priceless possessions only what you could put into one suitcase.

"You had better store your boxes in the mission house," advised Pastor Meleen, our superintendent. "There is no hope once the bandits and looters start work, but we will always feel we did our best if we store them all here."

So I packed up my boxes, the boxes that we had brought to Burma just four months before, our pictures, our photos, our linen, Mrs. Hare's darling dishes, our sweeper, our stand lamp. The weight in my heart and the lump in my throat grew heavier and bigger with each moment, and as I shut the lid on little Peter's tin train and Verna May's baby doll, I felt as though I had conducted a funeral. I felt like the undertaker, the preacher, the mourners, all in one. There were still three boxes that had not been unpacked yet. I might as well have a grand funeral while I was about it. I wanted to take one last, loving glance. My hand trembled as I lifted the lid. There they lay, so beautiful and bright, seven new brass band instruments, given by friends and loved ones in America and Australia for my famous jungle band. There was the E flat tuba that had never been played yet. There lay the euphonium, the two trombones, and the three silver-plated cornets. What sacrifice they represented. What possibilities! But it was too painful. I closed the box quickly and turned to peep into the others. My books, the cream of my library. My music, a collection of band music, choir music, and quartet music, and my file, a lifelong collection of clippings, a story, a poem, a gem for every occasion! How could I part with it all! My throat choked, my tears fell. I closed the boxes quickly, ran down into the highway, called a cartman, and lovingly and tenderly interred them in the mission house.

Hardly had I finished, when our next-door neighbor called at the foot of the stairs, "Mr. Hare, we are leaving for India by land route to Akyab. My brother and his family are with me, but we can only carry a suitcase and bed bundle each, and I have to leave everything in my house, but, Mr. Hare, that doesn't matter so much, but my car. Won't you please accept my car?" Her voice trembled. "I can't take it. I can't sell it. I can't bear to think of the enemy using it. Husband and I want you to take it. Use it as long as you can," then pointing a cold finger at me she added, "but if ever you have to abandon it, you take a gallon of gasoline and pour over it and set fire to it."

She turned quickly away to hide her sorrow, and left

me too bewildered for words. Although I could not fully believe it, we now had two cars to four men. This meant a few more valuables, and each of us packed another suitcase.

The next day, as I drove to ambulance duty in my newly acquired car, I found Dr. and Mrs. Walker, Pastor Sargent, and Pastor Johanson, from the Delta Mission, in serious council at the mission house.

"What's the news?" I asked cheerfully.

"Haven't you heard?" they replied woefully. "Singapore is gone."

"Singapore!" I could say no more.

"And the Delta Burmese are so openly hostile that the commissioner has ordered us to go," they added, and while I went toward my ambulance station, the rest of the men worked all night storing our missionaries' goods and the city clinic equipment in the mission house.

The next day Dr. and Mrs. Walker, Pastor Sargent, and Pastor Johanson left for Myaungmya by river boat, hoping to go up the coast via Akyab to Chittagong in a country sailing boat, and thence to Calcutta by rail. Since this plan provided another car for our final evacuation group, we were able to add to our own things the most essential office records. This in turn gave birth to a new hope, that we might be able to establish mission headquarters at Maymyo in northern Burma.

The following day, February 17, the enemy crossed the Bilin River, bringing them within eighty miles of the city. Pastor Christensen spent every spare moment devotedly visiting the few remaining church members, helping them to plan their getaway.

"I think I'll have them all out by Sabbath," he replied

wearily as I stopped by February 18 on my way to ambulance duty once more. "There are just three or four families left. The military is taking care of one, and the others plan to go soon."

Things looked different as I signed in that night. Only two drivers reported for duty.

"What's the matter, chief?" I queried.

"Matter?" he almost growled. "The St. John's Ambulance has been dismissed, and everybody has been told to go."

"No one has told me yet," I protested.

"I'm telling you now," he said bluntly, "and if you take my advice you'll go quickly. Don't you know the enemy could be here any time, and once they get here no one will get out."

"Well, chief," I replied, "we can't leave tonight, so I'll stay on duty with you. Then maybe in the morning we will be able to get away," and, hoping to read more about it in the paper the next morning, as I went off duty I went to the corner and shouted, "Paper." But the paper boy wasn't there. Thinking he was just a little late, I drove around by the press, poked my hand out of the window and called, "Paper. Paper." But no paper boy came. Soon an Indian workman came over and, with the whites showing all around the pupils of his eyes, he said, "No paper anymore, Sahib. We were paid two months' wages last night and told to go jildy, and we are going jildy."

"Now, *jildy* is a good Indian word which means "quick" or a little quicker than quick, if you can comprehend that, and when he told me he was going jildy, something in my heart seemed to tell me it was time for us to go jildy too. I drove directly to the mission house. Mr. Meleen, our superintendent, Mr. Christensen, the church pastor, and Mr. Baldwin, one of our teachers, were there. I told them what I had learned during the night, and added, "I'm ready to go right now. I think our time has come."

"Well," said Mr. Meleen, "let's ring up the consul and ask his advice. We don't want to leave too late, but we would feel foolish if we ran away before we had to."

He picked up the telephone, but the telephone was dead. The telephone company had been dismissed during the night, and the workers had been told to go.

"Oh, well," he said, "we'll drive around to see the consul."

We found his offices locked, and on the door was the notice,

"MOVED TO MAYMYO."

"Oh, well then, yes—I think it is time for us to go too," consented Mr. Meleen. "We'll dismiss the office boys today."

"And I have two families that I will get onto the afternoon river boat for Bassein," added Mr. Christensen. "Then we can all leave tomorrow."

During the rest of that day we learned via the "Grapevine Telephone Company" that military headquarters had moved out, and that government headquarters had moved out. The post offices were closed and had moved out. The bankers and the merchants were closed and had moved out. The hospitals dismissed their staffs, and by evening Rangoon was a madhouse of tangled traffic.

The streets were jammed for blocks and blocks with cars and busses and trucks, and at every gasoline pump there was rioting as men fought and struggled for the last drop of gasoline available in old Rangoon.

178

To make matters worse, Mr. Christensen came in that evening and shouted, "Bad news. Bad news."

We hastily found easy chairs and relaxed in them (for this, we have found, is the easiest way to "take it"); then we called, "All ready! Tell us the worst in the first mouthful!"

"I couldn't get my last two families onto the boat," he groaned. "We were there in plenty of time, but there wasn't even room to hang on the outside. Over two hundred passengers were left on the wharf, yelling and screaming to go."

He waited a moment while our heads began to swim, then turning to me he said, "Mr. Hare, you help me in the morning. The boat from Bassein gets in about 8:30 A.M., and though it doesn't leave till 4 P.M., we could get our folks on that boat while they are still unloading, and they wouldn't mind waiting all day till 4 P.M. to go. They will be glad enough to go any way."

By ten o'clock Friday morning, we had them nicely settled on the river boat for Bassein. We shook hands, commended them to the mercy of God, and were just about to leave them to come back to the mission house and begin our own evacuation journey, when an official came running down to the wharf, and, putting his hands to his mouth, shouted out, "No boats running today! No boats running today! All boats canceled! All boats canceled! Military has taken over all boats. All passengers off, please! All passengers off!"

And someday I want to forget what happened during the next few hours.

Have you ever read in the good old Book about those who wait till the summer is gone and the harvest is past, then cry, "Too late, too late, and we are not saved"?

I've heard it.

Have you ever read of the weeping and wailing and gnashing of teeth?

I've seen it, and it is the most painful sight that human eyes could see and the most awful sound that human ears could hear.

For hours we helped screaming, hysterical women from the boat, took them to their homes and tried to comfort them when there was no comfort.

Then we came back to the mission house and tried to plan what could be done next. But there seemed to be no plans. There was only one thing on which we were unanimous. We were going to find a way out for our last two families, or we were going to stay with them and share their fate.

How could we stand before our churches at home, who have supported foreign missions so faithfully for years, and tell them that we fled for our lives leaving two families to their fate.

We couldn't do it—we wouldn't do it.

While we canvassed the district for empty seats in outgoing cars or trucks, we sent Mr. Baldwin to the railway station to make inquiries about trains, and by evening he came with the glad news, "The military have taken over all the trains. There are to be two public evacuee trains north and two west tomorrow. All we have to do is to get our folks to the station and through the gates, and they can get off all right. But, gentlemen," he added, "before you feel too happy, read this," and, taking a poster from his pocket, he unfolded it, and we read, "Civilians of Rangoon are hereby given forty-eight hours' notice to get out of the city. Forty-eight hours from now the city will be closed, and all vehicles found therein after that period of time will be destroyed. By order, Commissioner of Police."

For a moment we felt decidedly queer. We were thinking of concentration camps—that maybe we had left it till it was too late also. But there was one chance. We might possibly get our last two families to the station that evening so that they could board the evacuee train the next morning. We ran around and laid our plans before them. No good waiting till morning. They must somehow get to the station and sleep there that night. Since they were willing for anything, we put them into our cars and drove toward the station. Ordinarily the Grand Central Station is a beautiful place, surrounded with gardens and lawns and parking places, but, as we neared it at this midnight hour, our hearts sank. For acres and acres the lawns, gardens, sidewalks, and parking places round about were covered with the sleeping, resting forms of thousands of Indians and Chinese, who hoped to go by the evacuee trains the next day. How could we hope to get through this mass of people and through the gates onto the platform! As we stepped in and out and over the sleeping forms, we caught sight of the soldier guards at the gates, with bayonets set. We had no authority, we had no passes, no tickets, no permits! I've done some earnest praying in my day, but I've never prayed harder than I prayed that night as I led that little single-file procession. And I always will believe that we witnessed a miracle that night, for what do you think I saw? What do you think I heard? As we came nearer and nearer, the English guard recognized the ambulance uniforms that Mr. Baldwin and I were both wearing, and we heard him call to his mate on the other side of the gate and say, "'ullo, buddy! 'ere come the marines. Open up!"

And the gates opened up, and we went in. A little later Mr. Baldwin took the office boys down. Again the gates opened, and in they went. I was going to say that they slept on the platform that night, and as the train pulled in next morning, they scrambled for a place, but nobody wanted to sleep. They spent the rest of that night praising God for opening a way of escape. Assured by the guards that they would have no difficulty in getting the train, we again commended them to the mercy of God and came home for a few hours' rest before starting on our journey the next morning.

And that day was Sabbath, February 21, 1942, a day long to be remembered in the history of Rangoon. Oh, what a day that was! I rose early, made my bed, and patted it good-by—my good old Yankee bed. Then I went into the kitchen, ate my breakfast, then patted my stove good-by—a brand new kerosene range we had just had shipped from America. Then I waved good-by to the Frigidaire, the rugs on the floor, the pictures on the wall, and the chairs around the room, and, choking with emotion, I turned the key in my door and cried "Good-by, home sweet home," and hurried down to the mission house.

There the other three men were doing their final packing. We said little, for we preferred to suffer in silence. Finally our cars were loaded. We were all ready to go. We entered the house of God for the last time. Our hearts breaking, but strangely subdued and resigned, we sang our last song.

> "When through fiery trials thy pathway shall lie,
> My grace all sufficient shall be thy supply;
> The flame shall not hurt thee; I only design
> Thy dross to consume and thy gold to refine.

"The soul that on Jesus doth lean for repose,
I will not, I will not desert to his foes;
That soul, though all hell should endeavor to shake,
I'll never, no never, no never forsake."

The preacher prayed his last prayer. The Bible was closed on the altar, and with the pews all emptied of men, we closed the door.

Stunned to tearful silence, we opened the gates of the mission compound and were just about to drive out and take our places in that never-ending line of pathetic evacuees when, for the ninety-second time, the air-raid signal sounded, and another mighty battle took place right overhead. Then, while waiting for the all clear to sound, we witnessed another tragedy of the last days of Rangoon. Though the battle was raging overhead, but few took heed. The city was fast emptying, the roads were filled with an endless throng of people, walking, cycling, riding in rickshas, gharries, carts, and cars and, as the innocent sufferers of this mad war moved out, we could not but be struck with the appearance of smaller groups walking in. Their hair was cut short; their shirts and longyis were all the same, and new; their legs were bowed. They reminded us somewhat of the groups of criminals we had occasionally seen working outside of the jail, with their legs bowed by the shackles they wore. Still they came. Could they be?

"Say there, friend!" we called to a well-dressed man passing by. "Do you have any idea who these men could be?"

"Only too much do I know," he replied with a heavy heart. "This is the last day, you know. Tomorrow the city will be closed. The keepers of the zoo wanted to leave, and as there was no one left to feed the animals, they shot the lions and tigers and other wild beasts, and let the others go. The wardens at the lunatic and leper asylums opened the doors and let their poor unfortunate inmates go where they would, so that they themselves might get away. Over at the prison, the jailers wanted to go, and because there would be no one left to look after the criminals, they took off their shackles, gave them each a new outfit, and then opened the doors of the prison for the three thousand criminals to walk into town."

"We have surely come upon evil days," I commented.

"Evil days! You're right, and it's God have mercy on us all," he replied sadly.

After seeming hours the all clear sounded. In silence and with heavy hearts we slowly glided out onto the highway and carefully took our place in the fleeing procession of homeless evacuees from Rangoon.

Evil spirits gloated over the scene. If they had their way these men who had been gathering jewels for Christ's kingdom should all miserably perish. Could the God in whom they trusted deliver them?

CHAPTER

9

Out of the Iron Furnace

✄✄✄✄✄✄✄✄✄✄

"But the Lord hath taken you, and brought you forth out of the iron furnace . . . to be unto Him a people of inheritance, as ye are this day." Deuteronomy 4:20.

In Another Two Hours We Had Loaded Our Cars and Were on Our Way

Out of the Iron Furnace

>+><+><+><+><+><+><+><+><

MILE AFTER MILE we picked our way through indescribable scenes of suffering and woe before we came to a break in the crowd. Past groups of burning cars and trucks, which were being destroyed because there was no more petrol available to move them; past hundreds and hundreds of crying babies and little children dragging at the clothes of their parents; past hundreds of exhausted wanderers lying on the roadside; past scores of feeble ones being dangled along in blankets hanging from bamboo poles, or being piggy-backed, or otherwise carried on the shoulders of the stronger ones; past hundreds and hundreds of weary travelers drinking from slimy mud pools in the rice fields; till our hearts were wrung dry, and there was not a tear left to sympathize with the discouraged, despairing ones we met that day. And the next day it was just as bad, but the pain was intensified by the news that two hundred hapless evacuees, hoping to rest their weary feet for a few short miles, had met a tragic death when they climbed onto the roof of the night evacuee train, and, as the train sped off into the darkness, were swept off by a low overhung bridge. Their dead bodies were strewn along the railway line for miles.

At Prome, one hundred and eighty miles from Rangoon, we parted with those who were escaping on foot. Their path led across the river and thence across the hills through Akyab to Chittagong. Ours lay northward through Meiktila along the road to Mandalay and Maymyo, where our north Burma workers had made temporary headquarters in our nursing home there.

You can hardly imagine the sense of relief that filled our hearts when, on the evening of the second day, we neared the little town of Taungdwingyi. How reassuring it was to be nearly three hundred miles from the bursting bombs in Rangoon. Yet haunting this assurance was the dread of not finding a good place to camp. Our water pots had been empty since four o'clock, and we had been looking for the green pastures and the still waters, or even a village well, but finding nothing, we had pushed on to this little town. It was 8:30 P. M. and dark.

"Could you give us any idea where we might camp?" we asked a policeman at the crossroads.

"Try the high school," he answered kindly. "A company of the Royal Air Force is there. It is evacuating the military ladies, and may have room."

We turned to the right, drove a block or two, and soon a pleasant-voiced captain said, "Come right in, gentlemen. You are welcome. Just park your cars over there near the trucks. The building is filled with the women, but I suppose you won't mind sleeping on the ground with us!"

"Not in the least," we replied cheerily. "We are prepared for anything, and if you could just tell us where the water is, we'll have supper ready in no time."

"Water? Oh, yes, the faucet is just outside the gates, to the left."

"I'll get the water while you make camp," said Mr. Baldwin, as he rattled off into the darkness with our three empty water pots. But in a minute he rattled back again.

"I'm sorry, gentlemen," he said dismally, "but this little town has water rationing, and the faucets were turned off at sunset and will not be turned on till sunrise, and till then there's not a drop of water to drink anywhere."

We had been thirsty since four o'clock, but now that we knew there was no water, our tongues swelled and speech was almost beyond us. No water! We must have water! Every other comfort was forgotten, and, standing there in the darkness, we prayed, "Lord, you promised our bread and our water would be sure. Never mind the bread, Lord. We have plenty of bread, but we must have water."

Just then out of the darkness we heard a voice call, "Well, I declare! If it isn't Pastor Christensen! What are you doing here?"

"Same as you," he replied laconically, walking into the darkness with his hand out. The next minute he shouted back, "Well, if it isn't Mr. Hern, a young man who was attending our tabernacle meetings in the city."

"And what are *you* doing here?" we asked as he walked into our circle.

"I'm fleeing for my life, gentlemen," he confided.

And I added, "So are we, but we are going to die of thirst before morning. We can't get any water!"

"Water!" he said. "We knew the water was rationed here, so we got a couple of cans full before it was turned

189

off, and say, don't bother cooking any supper. The boys have just finished dinner, and there is a whole pot of rice left and all kinds of curry." In a minute or two it was before us. You should have heard us give thanks for our bread and water that night.

It was still too dark to recognize people when we began to stir in the morning. We packed up our cars, checked our oil and petrol, and I realized sadly that I would have to begin using my five-gallon can of kerosene which I had brought along for emergency, as I had burned up more gasoline than I had expected to do, in evacuating our last two families. I realized now that I did not have enough gasoline to do the two hundred more miles to Maymyo.

"When you get a few miles along the road," I almost whispered to Mr. Meleen, who was to lead our caravan, "stop for a moment while I put in a couple of gallons of kerosene. It will be better to begin using a mixture now than to have to run on straight kerosene later."

I had only whispered my request, but hardly were the words out of my mouth when a deep bass voice boomed pleasantly beside me, "Gettin' low in petrol, buddy? I think I could let y' have a tin."

Looking up in surprise, I saw one of the big truck drivers, and stammered my sincere thanks. While I fumbled for the funnel, he brought over a two-gallon can of gasoline.

"Do y' think it'll hold another?" he said as the first tin drained into the tank.

"It sure will," I replied hopefully.

"Well, I think I could let y' have another one," was his friendly answer, and in went the second tin.

Now, I don't claim that this was a miracle, but my simple faith compels me to believe that God had something to do with giving me four gallons of petrol when we hadn't passed a drop for sale anywhere in that three-hundred-mile journey from Rangoon.

About fifty miles along the road Mr. Christensen waved us to the side of the road. "There's a horrible noise in my left rear wheel," he said. "Would you mind listening while I start up."

We listened, but he didn't start up. We said, "Do that again," for we wanted to make sure before we told him what we thought it was. He did it again, and we said, "Christensen, you never will start up again, for your wheel flange has broken off from the hub." To make sure, we took the wheel off.

"Just what I feared," groaned Mr. Christensen. "I had that welded once before, and now it's broken again."

"And there's no garage on the next corner either," added Mr. Meleen.

For a few moments we were very grave, for we all knew that there was only one thing to do, but no one wanted to say it. We had passed one hundred and sixty abandoned, burned cars along the way, and it seemed that Mr. Christensen's faithful old car would have to join this ill-fated company of derelicts. The rule for an abandoned car in the time of war was that it must be burned, and it's hard to tell a companion that he must take a gallon of gasoline, pour it over his car and set fire to it.

"If only we could get him to Yenangyaung," at last sighed Mr. Baldwin. "There is a bus running from there to Meiktila."

"I've got it," said Mr. Meleen. "Yenangyaung is only thirty-two miles away. We two will drive on, find a place to camp, unload one car, come back and pick up Mr. Christensen's load, take him to Yenangyaung and get a bus. In this way we can save all our luggage."

The more we thought of it, the more feasible the plan seemed. Off we drove, therefore, leaving Mr. Christensen and his lame car on the roadside. By five o'clock in the evening we had unloaded and made camp on the cement tennis court of the American Club at Yenangyaung.

"I'll take the car back for Mr. Christensen," volunteered Mr. Baldwin. "It will be dark by the time I get there, but we'll come back first thing in the morning. We will be here by nine o'clock for sure."

We readily agreed, for he was the youngest man of our group, and, while he went back, Mr. Meleen and I gave ourselves up to the luxury of a bath and shave, followed by a real meal at the club and a night's rest on the cement court.

Early the next morning we were up checking the cars as they came along the highway, but by nine o'clock the car had not returned. At ten o'clock there was no sign of it, and Mr. Meleen groaned, "I'm afraid something has happened. Let's unload your car, Mr. Hare, and go back and see what the trouble is." Unloading my little English Standard, and leaving our goods in the care of a faithful servant, we started back. Carefully we looked over each approaching car, but the car we looked for was not on the road. At last we reached the place where we had left Mr. Christensen, but there was no sign of either his or Baldwin's car anywhere. We could see the marks of the wheels at the roadside, but cars and men had vanished. Here indeed was a mystery, and our anxiety lest some dire misfortune had happened to our companions increased.

Crossing the road a little to the south, I approached a

Burmese hut and inquired, "Could you tell us anything about the man and the car we left here yesterday?"

"Oh, yes," was the reply. "A bus towed both of them to Mergwey this morning."

"Both of them!" we puzzled. "To Mergwey!" and the mystery grew deeper.

Since Mergwey was only a small place about three miles off the highway, we decided to go there. "Could you tell us if ——" we began to inquire of the native policeman we met as we came into the main street of this little river town, but we said no more, for there a little ahead of us was Mr. Christensen and his crippled car. "What —— Where ——"

"Wait. Wait," he interrupted smiling. "It's quite a story. Mr. Baldwin got stuck in the sandy river last night and in getting away burnt out the clutch plate. It was nine o'clock before he got here, and this morning neither of us could budge an inch, so, hearing that there was a bicycle repair shop in Mergwey, we got towed in to see what we could do. The man is working on the clutch plate and believes it will be ready by evening. I won't have to burn my car here. I can store it, you know, and there's almost a hope that I can come back when the war is over and pick up my car again." He paused to let us comprehend it all.

"Oh!" we at last sighed together. "Evening!" Then an idea came to my mind, and I thought out loud. "If we are to be held up till evening, why not take the broken hub to Yenangyaung and try to get it welded! There are oil fields and oil companies there, and I'm sure I saw two garages there. Maybe we can ——"

"Sure we can," shouted Mr. Christensen triumphantly. "If there is a garage there, we certainly can get my hub welded." And within an hour I was on my way back to Yenangyaung with the broken hub in my car.

"I have a broken hub here that I would like to have welded," I said, going into the first garage.

"So have I," replied the manager, "and lots of other things to weld too, but my welder evacuated three weeks ago, and there's not a welder left in town."

Not liking the way the man talked, I went to the next garage and said, "How about getting a little welding job done?"

"Welding!" the manager called in surprise. "No hope at all. All welders have evacuated."

I didn't like the way that man's voice sounded either, and I walked away wondering what I could do.

That morning we had become acquainted with the storehouse manager of the Nat Sing Oil Company, Mr. William Lawson, a very kindly English gentleman, and I said to myself, "It's no use wasting time looking for garages and welders. Mr. Lawson will know if it is possible to get this hub mended or not, and maybe he knows of an old wreck from which we can pick up another wheel." I hunted him up and explained our predicament.

He listened but sadly shook his head. "No welders in town, Mr. Hare. They told you quite right, and there are no Standard wrecks around here. We all drive Fords and Chevrolets up this way," he said. "But look, Mr. Hare, just knock on that door and speak to the boss."

Now, I needed a welder, not a boss, but because Mr. Lawson was a kindly, interested man, I knocked on the door as he told me to do and was ushered into the presence of a very pleasant Indian gentleman. As I explained the predicament of four missionaries with three cars, two of

194

which were disabled, I saw him tap a bell. A servant appeared to whom the boss gave a signal, and by the time I was finished Mr. Lawson stood beside me. "Mr. Lawson," said my unexpected benefactor, "I think it would pay Mr. Hare to go out to our oil field twenty miles away. There are no welders here, but our boys could fix that for him in a very little while. Won't you take him out to our workshop, Mr. Lawson?"

I couldn't believe it. It seemed like a dream, but I stammered my thanks and made my exit, and in about an hour we were out at the oil field. We pulled up in the midst of derricks and piles of iron pipe, and I heard Mr. Lawson shout as he went to the workshop door, "Stop work, boys. A rush order from the boss." And five Indian mechanics hovered over our broken hub while Mr. Lawson and I reclined in easy chairs and talked about fulfilling prophecy.

In half an hour the hub was mended and put in my car.

"How can I thank you, Mr. Lawson?" I said, shaking him warmly by the hand. "How much is the bill?"

"It's a pleasure to help you," he said. "There is no bill. Just drop in and thank the boss."

I dropped in and thanked the boss, you may be sure, and as I sped off to where I had left the other men up to their elbows in grease, thirty-five miles away, I took time out to thank someone else, for I will always believe that there was a loving God besides that pleasant Indian boss, who had something to do with getting that hub welded.

"It's fixed! It's fixed!" I yelled, as I pulled up suddenly beside the men in Mergwey.

Mr. Christensen could hardly believe his eyes. He grabbed the hub, turned it over and over, then raced off to

195

his car, and in half an hour we heard him purring around the block.

"It's better than ever it was before," he cried as he finally drove up to us. "It's just like getting the old car back from the grave."

The work on the other car, however, proved to be a longer job than we expected, and it was 2 P.M. the next day before our complete caravan started off for Yenang-yaung again, but three whole cars left Mergwey with everybody and everything on board.

We spent one more delightful night on our cement tennis court, and early the next morning packed up and got ready to leave on the next stage of our journey.

"Let's call in and thank Mr. Lawson again," I suggested, and, while we chatted hopefully over the latest radio bulletin, I whispered, "Of course, Mr. Lawson, we know the government has commandeered all the gasoline, but we were just wondering if we could find a drop or two anywhere before we left."

His eyes twinkled. "Quite right, Mr. Hare," he replied. "The government has commandeered all the gasoline—that is, nearly all the gasoline, but we still have a little left. Just come along with me," and he took us to a garage off the highway and filled our tanks and every empty can we had, and when we pulled out of Yenangyaung, we had more gasoline than when we left Rangoon five days before.

During that day, as we traveled toward Meiktila on the road to Mandalay, we had ten unbridged rivers to cross. The descent into the rivers and the ascent on the other side were so steep and perilous that we held our breath as we labored down one side and up the other.

Often we had to wait a half hour while a tow car pulled

cars up the other side. Once we had to wait more than an hour while a wrecking crew pushed a big truck to one side in the river. The truck had climbed halfway up the opposite bank when an axle broke, and the truck had come crashing down into the river again. I tell you, we formed the habit of waiting for each other after crossing each river and, as we would sigh with relief that another river had been crossed, Mr. Christensen would say, "I tell you, gentlemen, I'm so glad my hub broke away down there near Mergwey. If it had broken halfway up this riverbank, what would we have done?"

And no sooner would Mr. Christensen finish his speech than Mr. Meleen would add, "And I tell you, gentlemen, I am glad my clutch burnt out down yonder in the sand! It never could have pulled me out of this river."

And can you believe it? By the time we had reached Meiktila that evening, we had actually been praising God all day long for the broken hub and the burnt-out clutch. Time was when I thought that all things working together for good, meant water when there was no water and gasoline when there was no gasoline, but I know now that when God says, "All things work together for good," He means broken hubs and burnt-out clutches too!

At Meiktila, where our fine training school was established, we found our faithful Burmese and Karen press workers still carrying on. The school buildings had been taken over by the government since January 1, but they had permitted us to continue using our press. We rejoiced to find the Sabbath school lessons for the coming quarter and the *Watchman* magazine all off the press and ready for mailing to Upper Burma.

After studying the situation with the workers and help-

197

ing them to make plans in the event war reached them, we drove on the next day to Mandalay and up the hill to Maymyo, our north Burma headquarters. Here we were glad to find Pastor Wyman, Pastor Baird, and Pastor Skau and his family, and it seemed like heaven to be with friends again, and to have a home where we could bathe and shave and wash our clothes, and then lie down to sleep in a real bed.

Hoping almost against hope that we could stay on in Upper Burma, we listened eagerly to the record of events as it was broadcast day by day.

The radio gave little real news, but to the last day spoke hopefully and optimistically about holding Rangoon. Other news brought through by stragglers, however, was not so cheerful. Led by the three thousand liberated convicts, bands of Burmese had descended from everywhere upon the deserted city to loot and to plunder. Watson and Company, one of the great general stores, was left bare, without even a handkerchief. Coombs and Company, the jewelers, were treated the same way, and the cloth bazaar was ransacked and burned. Trying to curb this shameful state of affairs, a company of soldiers challenged three hundred of the ruffians in Rowe and Company's store, and when the looters refused to replace their plunder, the soldiers shot them all, but this did not stop it. In bullock wagons they carted furniture and clothing from the homes of the rich, then burned what was left. Poor Rangoon! Was ever a proud capital so humiliated. God only knows what happened to our homes and belongings which we were forced to leave behind.

On the ninth of March the great Burma Road was cut at Pegu, and the enemy forces were reported to be racing across to the Irrawaddy. That night the Japanese army entered Rangoon, and we knew it was time to leave Burma—if we could.

Mr. Baldwin had been advised to proceed to India with another group as soon as we arrived in Maymyo; consequently, early the next morning Mr. Baird, Mr. Wyman, and I, in Mr. Baird's Ford Vanette, and Mr. Meleen and Mr. Christensen, in Dr. Walker's car, with each car carrying thirty gallons of petrol, started off down the hill to Mandalay. This left only Mr. Skau and his family, who were planning to fly out a little later. At Mandalay we had been told we could put both cars on the river boat and unload them right at Pakokku the next morning. Pakokku was one hundred and fifty miles downstream on the west bank of the Irrawaddy and was the beginning of the cart track which showed as an irregular dotted line on our maps. And this was the only possible way out of Burma left open to us. We went at once to the steamship agent in Mandalay and said cheerfully, "We have two cars we would like to ship to Pakokku."

"Sorry, gentlemen," he replied. "There's no hope in the world. All our big passenger boats that can carry cars are more than a week overdue. Evidently someone's got them. We hope it's our own troops and not the enemy."

"Oh-o-oh," we sighed as our hearts sank at the prospect.

"I could put one car on the little ferry to Mingyan tonight if that's any good to you."

"But that's still on the Japanese side of the river, isn't it?" "Yes, but it would save you one hundred miles of gasoline, and Java fell this morning, gentlemen, and the enemy made thirty-five miles north of Pegu, where they cut the Burma Road."

"Thank you," we breathed. "We'll put Mr. Meleen's car on tonight's boat."

Mandalay was hot and dusty. The Burmese were openly insolent, and it was 10 P.M. when we finished loading Mr. Meleen's car on the Mingyan boat and got back to the Ford. I can't remember suffering from thirst so much in all my life before. The crowds of evacuating Indians made the work almost impossible, and now, almost exhausted, we found our way to the home of one of our church members, and drank and drank and drank while we studied our next move together. We couldn't wait another day. Things were happening too fast. It was one hundred miles by road to Mingyan, and we would need more gasoline.

"What hope is there of getting any gasoline here?" we said to our friend, Mr. Isaac.

"No hope of getting any government gasoline at all," he replied with emphasis, "but I did hear of some bootleg gas for sale in the Chinese section. You might run around there and inquire."

We acted on his suggestion, but the Chinese merchant said, "Just sold my last drop. I wish I had ten thousand gallons more. I could make my fortune."

"How much did you sell it for?" we asked.

"Four-fifty a gallon," he grinned, and we would have even been glad to buy ten gallons at that price.

While it was still dark, we felt our way out of the blacked-out old capital of Mandalay. For a long time no one spoke. The future seemed dark, and we were discouraged and blue.

"Well, I wonder where we will be this time tomorrow morning?" I groaned at last.

And Mr. Wyman replied a little more cheerfully, "I'm

sure I don't know *where* we will *be,* but I can tell you *what* we will be *saying.*"

"Even that would help a lot," I assured him. "What do you think we will be saying?"

"Every day we have not been able to see one day ahead," he answered, "but every day we've been able to say, 'Hitherto hath the Lord helped us,' and I fully expect to be saying it again this time tomorrow morning," with this heartening reminder we reconsecrated ourselves to the service of God, and recounting His providences, pressed on.

By noon we reached the town of Mingyan, a typical Burmese town, on the riverbank in the monsoon season when the river is six miles wide, but now nearly three miles from the edge of the rough, hot, dusty, sandbank where the ferryboat pontoons were.

"Going to the pontoons?" asked a bullock-cart man who drove up as we were standing there.

"Yes, but we have a car," we replied.

"Car! You can't go by car. I've never seen a car go over that sand. I've never heard of a car going over that sand. It can't be done and you can't do it," he replied vehemently. "Better get into my cart and I'll take you there."

We thought for a moment and then Mr. Baird said, "And I'll look for some grease and oil while you are making arrangements to cross the river."

Assuring Mr. Baird that we wouldn't be long, we jumped into the bullock wagon and rumbled off over the furnacelike sandbank to the edge of the river.

"I'm sorry, gentlemen," said the steamer agent there. "I can give you no hope of ever getting your cars to Pakokku. The small launch to Pakokku cannot take cars, and the large steamers from Prome are many days overdue. We hope the

201

government has taken them and not the enemy. Of course, you might cross the river by canoe and walk to the border. It is only three hundred miles from here."

"He was sympathetic enough," I said to Mr. Wyman as we walked slowly outside.

"But you can't take cars across the river on sympathy," he added dryly. "What we need is to contact Moses for a little while or, if we could only find his rod, that might help."

We stood in the shade of the pontoon. It was scorching hot. It was dusty. Our clothes were wet with perspiration. The pulses in our temples beat wildly, but our hearts were too heavy to think, our mouths too dry to talk.

"Let's not bother with Moses or his rod," I suggested. "It would take too long to hunt them up, but we can contact Moses' God—right now." As so often we had done, we lifted our hearts to God in prayer. When we opened our eyes and looked around, we noticed to our right fifty or sixty mat shacks, which sheltered innumerable bullock-cart drivers and their bullocks as they lazily rested during the heat of the day. At our backs was the mile-wide river swirling by. To our left, beyond the pontoons, were forty or more country boats, big and little, with their various cargoes of cotton and rice, loading and unloading. We eyed them in silence for a moment, then both broke out together, "Do you suppose we could tie a couple of those boats together and put some planks across ——!"

"That's the idea, the very idea," said Mr. Wyman, moving off. "Let's go and see."

Eagerly we began to canvass that line of boats, but our burden became no lighter.

"No, we're already hired to carry rice."

"Never heard of anything like that being done before. Never saw anything like that before. We're not going to do it."

"No, indeed! Think we want to be sunk!"

That's what they said as we went down the line, and the jeering crowd of antiforeign Burmese boatmen increased at every step. It was most uncomfortable to hear them whispering together about what they would do with a wheel or a tire or a suitcase. For they were so sure we were stuck, and would have to leave the cars behind, and go the rest of the way on foot. We were just about to give up, when a tall, jungly-looking man pushed into the crowd and said,

"What's this? What's this? Put a car on a boat! Of course I can."

"But we have two cars," I eagerly replied, turning to him.

"And I have two boats," he said.

"Then how much will you charge us to take us and our cars to Pakokku?" we asked.

"That's downstream. It will take us one day to get there and four days to get back. I'll do it for fifty-five rupees," he said.

We were so glad we nearly fainted, but it would have been unwise to agree to the price too quickly, so we threw up our hands, and went through the customary bickering, declaring that no living human mortal would ever dream of giving such a fortune for five days' work. But at last it was settled that he should provide the coolies to load and the planks to put the cars on for his price. Paying him twenty-five rupees advance to get the boats ready, we went off to tell Mr. Baird the good news.

"Good news!" we shouted as we saw Mr. Baird a block away in the town.

"More good news," he yelled back.

It sounded fine, but we wondered what good news he could possibly have that would compare to finding a way across the Irrawaddy.

"We've got a raft all ready to take us across the river," we announced with glee. Then we demanded, "Now what's yours?"

"Why," he explained, "I found some grease and oil. Then I sauntered over to the court, made friends with the officer who issues permits for gasoline, and believe it or not, he gave us a permit for six gallons on the two cars, and we now have just as much gas as when we left Mandalay."

We turned into a rice shop to celebrate our successes with a little food, then prepared to take the car across the sand to the pontoons.

"It couldn't be done. It never has been done. You can't do it," they said, but you know it's really wonderful what a Ford can do, especially if you can talk Ford language and know where to pat. We put our baggage into a bullock wagon. Mr. Baird sat at the wheel saying nice things to the car. I walked ahead, beckoning and coaxing it along. Mr. Wyman brought up the rear with an understanding push and an occasional pat, and in two hours we were there.

As we brushed the dirt from our faces and coughed the dust from our mouths, however, we were disappointed to see that the raft was nowhere to be seen. And when we found the boatman, and heard him say, "Aw, I didn't think you could get here," we began to wonder if he had promised to take us to Pakokku only to get the deposit. However there we were with the car. He couldn't lose face.

So we rolled up our sleeves and began to tie the boats together.

"We couldn't get planks," explained the boatman. "The only sawmill in the town was closed last week, and the owner has evacuated to the other side of the river, but we have sent a lad to the village to try to find some other planks and he should soon be here.

We waited for half an hour and said, "Where are the planks?"

"They are coming now," the boatman replied.

The ferry boat whistled a mile or two away, and again we asked, "Where are the planks?"

"They are coming. Oh, here they are. Here they are!" and a boy in a canoe came into sight with one plank twenty feet long, six inches wide and one and a half inches thick, and two planks about eight feet long, flat on one side and round on the other. Imagine as I could, I couldn't see a car riding on planks like that.

"Oh, but we'll prop them up with bamboos and tie them with ropes," said the boatman.

They did, and, as the ferry boat with Mr. Meleen, Mr. Christensen, and the car on board tied up at the pontoon, we drifted down alongside and displayed our raft with permissible elation.

Mr. Meleen was delighted with our idea, because they had gathered little hope of ever getting the cars any farther, as they came down the river.

"We'll get some more planks in the morning for the other car," we explained, "but it will be easier to load your car right from the steamer onto the raft rather than unload it onto the riverbank and then onto the raft."

"And they say the Japanese have come thirty-five miles

farther north today above Pegu and have reached Prome on the Irrawaddy."

"Then let's load your car right away," we urged.

The coolies swung the car into line with our planks. I stood at the end of one plank and Mr. Christensen stood at the end of the other, guiding Mr. Meleen at the wheel. Little by little the car neared the edge of the steamer. The front wheels balanced for a moment on the edge of nothing, then settled gently onto the planks across our country boats. They touched—the boats took the weight—the car rolled forward six inches. It was our big moment—six more inches—a little this way—success was just within reach—six more inches—a little that way—then an ominous crack! My heart sank. In my mind I already saw the boats and the car sinking to the bottom of the river. I closed my eyes in near collapse, but we didn't sink. I opened my eyes and found that instinctively the coolies had pulled back altogether. The wheels were just balanced on the edge of the steamer again. I gave one mighty shout. A score more rushed to the rescue, lifting and pulling, and the car rolled back onto the deck of the river boat.

"Better unload it on the riverbank in the morning," was all I could say to the captain, as I wiped the perspiration from my brow. Then in utter despair we poled ourselves back to our anchorage. May we never have to spend another night like that night at Mingyan. Too exhausted to go anywhere, we spread our beds on our luggage at the water's edge and lay down, but not to sleep. The insolent boat folk, who thought the five white men were trapped, talked loudly of what they would do with the cars and our baggage if we had to abandon them, and the mighty width of the river before us, together with the knowledge that every hour the enemy was advancing behind us made sleep impossible. Defeat was there making ugly faces at us all night long. I think I know now how the children of Israel felt at the Red Sea. I literally spent that whole night in prayer. I prayed that God would deliver us, that He would open a way for us to cross the river, that He would comfort our poor, weary, discouraged hearts, but no answer seemed to come till *four o'clock* in the morning. Then came an impression clear and distinct and persistent: "Go to the sawmill in the city, the sawmill that was evacuated. Go to the sawmill."

I awakened the boatman. "I've been talking to my God all night long," I said, "and He has told me to go to the sawmill in the city."

He looked at me in amazement for a moment, then said, "All right, Saya. Let us go."

We called a bullock wagon and started off. Dawn was just breaking as we stopped in front of the big gates of the sawmill in Mingyan.

"It's too early," I said. "The gates won't be ——" but they were open, and in we went.

As there seemed to be no one around, we went over to the timber racks at the end of the yard, and in about twenty minutes had selected four beautiful planks, eight and a half inches wide, two inches thick, and twenty-one feet long.

"Do you wish to buy some timber?" asked a polite young Burmese lad about fifteen years old, who by this time had walked toward us.

"Yes," I said. "When will the clerk come on duty?"

"The clerk will not come today, sir. We closed the mill last week and have evacuated to the other side of the river,

207

but I can sell you the timber. I am the son of the mill owner. You know, it is strange, but father woke me up about four o'clock this morning and sent me across to get some papers from the office, and I had just entered the door when your drove in.

And while he figured the price of those planks, I felt like taking my shoes from off my feet. The place where I was standing was holy with the presence of God.

"That will be ten rupees and eight annas," he said.

I paid the money gladly. It would have been worth it at ten times that amount. We loaded the timber and drove out of the yard. As we turned toward the riverbank where we were making our raft, the young man walked out after us, closed the gates and padlocked them, then turned in the opposite direction to go to where he would cross the river and return to his father. Silently we walked along behind our cart. I was loath to break that hallowed influence with my common words, and it was the Buddhist boatman who broke the silence at last. Touching my hand gently to attract my attention, he whispered, "Your God did help you, didn't He? Your God did help you, didn't He?"

We got the planks to the river at 9:30 A.M. Our raft was finished a half hour later. The loading of our two cars was complete in another two hours and by 11:45 we had weighed anchor and had begun our journey toward Pakokku on the other side of the river.

Oh, what delirious delight! We were on our way! We bathed, we ate, we slept, we rejoiced, we chlorinated some water and drank all we could hold. The sun gradually sank behind a gorgeous bank of golden glory. Such peace all around us, without and within. We slept on an island sand bar.

At 3 A.M. the Buddhist boatman awakened us and said, "See! The moon shines brightly. It is pleasant to travel when it is cool. If we start now we can unload in Pakokku before the heat of the day."

Eagerly we climbed onto our raft and pushed out into the current. The brilliant moonlight played hide and seek with the shadows of the coconut palms on the riverbank as we drifted gently downstream.

Because our hearts were again moved by the mighty deliverance our God had wrought, we burst spontaneously into singing:

> "All the way my Saviour leads me;
> What have I to ask beside?
> Can I doubt His tender mercy,
> Who through life has been my guide?
> Heav'nly peace, divinest comfort,
> Here by faith in Him to dwell!
> For I know whate'er befall me,
> Jesus doeth all things well."

Our voices blended into a harmonious male quartet, and we sang as we had never sung before. We were singing part of the Song of Moses and the Lamb, for our Saviour had made a way for us, a way through the waters of the old Irrawaddy. We sang till the boatmen could row no longer but listened spellbound to our songs of praise.

As we sang, I saw the old boatman touch his wife's hand, and, pointing tremblingly toward us, he whispered, "They are. They are. Those men are servants of the living God!"

The sun rose. In the distance we saw the gleaming pagodas of Pakokku. The smoke of the early-morning fires hung cloudlike over the housetops. Coming nearer, we saw

14 209

what appeared to be white clouds hovering on the river-bank below the city. We strained our eyes. The clouds were moving.

"What is it?" we asked the boatman.

"Thirty thousand Indian evacuees, waiting for boats to go up the Chindwin to the border," he replied, and thus, with a jolt, we were brought back to the reality of the fact that we, too, were fleeing for our lives.

.   .   .   .   .

"What can you tell us about the road to Tamu?" we inquired of the kindly faced district magistrate at Pakokku, to whose office we went as soon as we had unloaded our cars and cleaned up a little.

"Well, gentlemen," he replied in perfect English. "First I must tell you the road is closed, and I have been forbidden to issue any more permits for people to go that way. You see, plague and cholera have broken out in the evacuee camps, and the poor people are dying like flies, so no one is being allowed to travel over the road till the camps have been cleared up."

He paused for that little piece of information to soak in, and then went directly on, "Secondly, the road is terrible. Only one hundred miles are paved after a fashion, and the other two hundred are the roughest of cart tracks, with deep dust and ruts. But, gentlemen, cars and busses are getting through in about five days. I think Mr. Sargent and his party went that way about two weeks ago."

The name of Mr. Sargent startled us, for we had thought his party had gone via Akyab and the sea coast, but here was dependable news, for the magistrate knew our mission well and had bought books from Mr. Johanson, who was also in Mr. Sargent's party.

We were glad to know they were ahead of us. For a moment we commented on our satisfaction at knowing the other party was well on its way. Then seriously looking into the face of this Burmese official, Mr. Meleen inquired, "Sir, just what might happen if we chose to proceed without your permission?"

We gasped at such unbelievable frankness. He waited for a moment before replying, and I thought I saw almost a twinkle in his eye as he said, "You would have no difficulty with my policemen at this end. Of course, at Tamu they could make you come back, but I hardly think they would," and, lowering his voice, he added, "gentlemen, if I were in your position I think I would go without delay, but, of course, you understand I cannot give you a permit."

I knew now it was all a dream. Real people simply didn't talk that way, but there were the five of us sitting there. We felt like pinching each other to make sure. But it was real. The officer who could not give us a permit had advised us to go!

Then Mr. Baird made bold to ask, "Sir, how many gallons of gasoline do you think we would need for the trip?"

"Busses take eighty gallons," he said carefully. "I think a car could get through on forty."

"We have only thirty gallons each," Mr. Baird continued. "Could you possibly give us a permit to buy a little more?"

"Well, now—under the circumstances—I think—maybe I could," he replied. Reaching for his forms and his pen, he added, "Shall I write, say—twenty-two gallons?"

"Oh, thank you," we chorused, and feeling as if we

were still in a dream, we gave ourselves over to the happiness of a Sabbath day free from our recent anxiety, spent with a little group of our church members whom we found there. We were in Pakokku, on the other side of the river to the enemy. Hitherto had the Lord indeed helped us.

Our gasoline tanks were literally full and running over as we drove slowly out of Pakokku Sunday morning on the last long lap of our flight to India.

It took us till Thursday evening to travel the next three hundred miles to the Tamu Pass. We camped beside the still waters. We went through the valley of the shadow of death, where the poor Indians were dying of plague and cholera, feeling that God was with us and delivering us out of the fiery furnace. At Tamu we were forced to leave our cars and everything else but sixty pounds of necessities, and for the next four days we walked up and down over the pass into India. Slowly we crawled up—up, then painfully we crawled down—down—down, till at last we saw those high hills flatten out into the beautiful plain of Dinapur. Here busses and trucks awaited us at the beginning of the India road, and we were taken to the wonderful evacuation camp at Imphal. The next day busses and trucks took us 104 miles to the nearest railway station, and we were given free tickets to any part of India to which we wanted to go. At Calcutta news was awaiting us of the whereabouts of our families, and in a few more days we were together again.

In India we waited, hoping that the tide would turn and that we could go back again to Burma, to our home in Rangoon, and to the work and the people whom we loved. But the tide didn't turn.

On the ninth of April the Japanese bombed Colombo,

Cocanada, and Vizagapatam, thus spreading panic to the eastern coast of India.

Two days later the British proposals for home rule in India, brought by Sir Stafford Cripps in person, were rejected by the Indian congress. The same day our forces in the Philippines were forced to surrender, and Mandalay, the proud, glorious capital of Upper Burma, was razed to the ground—burned to ashes. The future looked dark.

On May 4, Lashio, the Burmese city on the northern end of the Burma Road into China, was taken, and in a few more days Major Stilwell and his tired, war-weary soldiers marched into India. Then we gave up hope of ever getting back to Burma and to the Karen people, whose language we knew so well.

Just when the future seemed darkest, the consul general in Bombay notified Americans of a ship that was westward bound, and told us to get ready. We didn't have to be told twice. We believed God was opening another way of escape. We got ready and waited. Finally one day the news came, and we were told to go aboard the luxurious troopship in Bombay. Twelve hundred passengers crowded on board and, for the next six weeks, with the ship blacked out every night, we zigzagged our way over the perilous waters of the ocean toward home sweet home.

To prevent any leakage of light, every night the portholes were screwed down till not a breath of air could enter. Every night the light bulbs were taken from our cabins. Among the twelve hundred passengers were four hundred and sixty-eight missionaries, representing twenty-one different mission boards, and every night they sat on the blacked-out deck and sang. I wish you could have heard them! Led by a band of two trumpets, two trombones, three violins, a saw, and two piano accordians, every night our theme song was—

> "Jesus, Saviour, pilot me
>   Over life's tempestuous sea;
> Unknown waves before me roll,
>   Hiding rock and treach'rous shoal;
> Chart and compass come from Thee;
>   Jesus, Saviour, pilot me."

And, as we sang, never was I more conscious that angel hands assisted our captain and his mates as they plotted our zigzag course through the dark night.

During that voyage, I need not tell where or when, one ship just one day ahead of us was torpedoed and sunk. Another ship one day behind us was torpedoed and sunk, but on and on we sailed.

We took on board crews of two torpedoed ships. Those three hundred men were so nervous that they went to bed every night fully dressed and even wore their life belts to meals. How glad they were to hear us singing that song!

On and on we sailed till one day in the clear morning sunshine we picked out the silvery wings of a Flying Fortress. Oh, how we cheered! It came closer and closer. It roared its welcome as it circled around us. How wonderful it felt to be found away out there, a tiny speck in the ocean, by one of our own flying ships. It told us what to do and where to go, and hovered over us through part of the night. Well that it did, for that night a sub chaser picked up the vibrations of our engines and was hot on our trail to see what we were. The plane above us saw the two ships nearing each other in the darkness, and dropped a "flaming onion" just in time to avert a collision.

Before the Flying Fortress left us, we were told that just

two days from home a little destroyer would join us and accompany us safely into port.

You should have heard those sailor boys cheer when one morning we woke up to find the little destroyer right beside us. It ran rings around us and zigzagged across our path, telling us where to go and what to do, while we yelled and cheered.

During that voyage we had some exciting moments, but I think the most exciting moment through which we ever lived came the morning after that little destroyer found us.

All during the voyage we had had lifeboat and life-belt drills, but they always came after the meals were over and the work done up. This morning, however, the alarm went while many of us were still at breakfast. We heard our gun crews rush to position. We heard them unveiling their guns and breaking their ammunition. Just then the stewards came running down the passageways shouting, "All life belts on! Everybody on deck! All life belts on! Everybody on deck! All life belts ———"

"Steward," I yelled, poking my head through the door as he passed. "Is this another practice, or is this the real thing?"

"I—don't—know," he mumbled, then continued shouting, "All life belts on! Everybody on deck!"

You should have seen us get up on deck! I never saw people move quicker in my life and just in time. There we saw the little destroyer to our right acting queerly—darting here, darting there, with all her men in battle array. In a split second we saw a signal given, and three depth charges were hurled overboard. There was a terrific explosion. The waters of the ocean bubbled and boiled, and into the curdling waters the little destroyer fired four shells from its rear rifle.

We stood there on deck with our hair standing on end and our ears twitching. The man to my right said he—distinctly—saw—the submarine—break up into splinters and sink to the bottom of the ocean. The man to my left said he saw nothing but water.

A sailor boy, one who had gone through a torpedo experience and had been in the ocean four days before he was picked up, lifted his hand and said, "Folks, don't be scared. That's just depth-charge practice. Just depth-charge practice."

"Oh, yeah!" said another sailor boy before the words were all out of the other fellow's mouth. "Oh, yeah!"

And, honestly, that's all we know, for Uncle Sam has never told us from that day to this whether it was the "real thing" or just a "depth-charge practice." All we know is that in half an hour the all clear sounded. We stroked our hair down flat, patted our ears, and, turning to each other, said,

"Did you see that? Did you hear that?"

"What did you see? What did you hear?"

But I'll tell you what we did know, and we knew it for sure. The next morning we were nearly home! We couldn't tell just where we were, for a fog blotted out the foreshore and Uncle Sam had never told us just where we were going to land, but there in the water beside us, drifting slowly to the rear, were the big red buoys indicating the channel to some port.

Such excitement! Everybody was on deck looking through the fog, counting away the big red buoys. Suddenly a sailor boy, with an air of superior knowledge, called,

"Folks, this is Baltimore! This is Baltimore! I came out of Baltimore five months ago, and there's a long row of red buoys just like this indicating the channel at Baltimore. Folks, this is Baltimore."

"Oh, yeah!" argued another. "Do you think Baltimore is the only port with red buoys indicating the channel? I've been in and out of New York five times during the past year, and there's a long line of red buoys just like this in New York Harbor. I'll say it's New York!"

"Wait a minute," shouted another. "I've been talking to some officers this morning, and, while, of course, they won't say for sure, one of them said he wouldn't be surprised if we landed at Charleston."

And so they argued, and the argument was getting hotter and hotter and more and more interesting, till it finally fell to a good old colored sailor boy to utter the right thing for all of us, for shouting high above the argument, he said, "Lan' sakes, folks. I don' care where it is. It can be Califrisco or San Franornia if it likes. Any ole place'll do me as long as it's the good old U.S.A."

And we yelled and we cheered, for that's exactly the way everybody felt.

We were still yelling and cheering and straining our eyes through the fog for a glimpse of some familiar object that could tell us where we were when suddenly from the forepart of our ship there arose a thunderous roar.

But nobody said, "What are they shouting for?" Nobody asked, "What do you suppose they have seen?" Instinctively everybody knew what it was. There was one mad rush to the port side of the ship, and then we all stood there laughing, crying, shouting, cheering, till we were hoarse; for there, rising from the fog at her feet, with her

217

head and her uplifted arm in the clear morning sunshine, stood "Old Liberty," and everybody knew where we were.

I wish you could have been on that boat that morning to have measured the emotion of those twelve hundred passengers and those three hundred rescued sailor boys, when they realized that God had brought them all safely home again.

Two dear old missionary ladies leaning on the rail just below me were singing "Praise God From Whom All Blessings Flow," and we all joined in, for we all felt just like that. Two others prayed aloud in words, thanking God for bringing us safely home again and everybody said, "Amen," for everybody felt just like that.

Just then a sailor boy pulled up a chair, mounted it, and, waving his hand affectionately toward "Old Liberty," he made a speech that I will remember as long as I live. "Hullo, Mother," he cried. "Here come some of your children. Oh, Mother, I'd like to jump right over to you and put my two arms around your neck and give you a big kiss, I would." And everybody cheered and everybody cried, for everybody felt just like that.

There stood beside me a sailor boy too overcome with emotion to say a word. For a long time he wiped his eyes and swallowed hard on that horrid lump that was choking the words out of him. Then, thumping me on the elbow, he said, "Do you know what I'm going to do the very first thing?"

I said, "No, my lad, I've no idea what you'll do first."

"Well, do you see that gangplank?"

"Yes," I said, "what are you going to do with it?"

"Well, I'm going off that gangplank, and I'm going to the nearest bit of land I can find, and I'm going to get down on my two knees and I'm going to kiss it, I am, and I don't care who sees me!"

And truly that's the way you feel when you know your God has brought you out of the fiery iron furnace, across the perilous deep, to home sweet home again.

Henry van Dyke said it for everybody when he wrote:

> "Oh, it's home again, and home again,
>   America for me!
> I want a ship that's westward bound
>   to plough the rolling sea,
> To the blessed Land of Room Enough
>   beyond the ocean bars,
> Where the air is full of sunlight
>   and the flag is full of stars."

Again our great God had triumphed gloriously. By His strong arm He had brought up every foreign worker and every church member that worked like a foreigner or talked like a foreigner out of the iron furnace. But what about Peter and Chit Maung and Po Shwey, the leaders of our three main missions, and the hundreds of believers who had to remain behind with them?

With the greatest of difficulty were we able to arrange for each worker to have an amount equal to about two months' wages, and that was *all* they had. Cut off without money, without clothes, without medicines, without the encouragement that the foreign workers could give, what would happen to them? Surrounded by hostile Buddhists shouting, "We will wash our hands in the blood of the Christians," encompassed by the fanatical pro-Japanese element, who suspected every Christian as a spy for the Allies, would the powers of evil succeed in blotting out the glad tidings of Christ, and put out the light forever?

219

CHAPTER

10

Gold Tried in the Fire

><><><><><><><><

"He shall sit as a refiner and purifier of silver: and He shall purify . . . and purge them as gold and silver." Malachi 3:3.

Even During the War Years Thara Peter Baptized New Converts

Gold Tried in the Fire

>+<>+<>+<>+<>+<>+<>+<>+<

THE WEEKS AND months of trial and persecution in Burma wore on to four long, dreary years of isolation, privation, nakedness, and starvation, before our missionaries could return and re-establish our contacts with them.

Brother Jim Baldwin was the first to reach them. Although we had advised him to go to India even before we left North Burma, he did not go. He started, but with every step away from "home" his heart grew heavier and heavier. He thought of the young men he had fathered as dean of our training school at Meiktila. He thought of the boys who had so often turned to him for comfort and advice, being at the mercy of a cruel godless enemy, and he could not go. Secretly he returned to central Burma, and connected with the army as welfare and air conducting officer to the Karen and Kachin paratroops. As the battle went against them the Karens and Kachins succeeded in getting through to India with Stilwell.

In November 1943, Jim was made an honorary chaplain and was with the Karen soldiers on the Arakan front, on the Chin hills, and in the Chindwin valley. In his contacts he was able to give us the first fragmentary news of destruction of our mission property and loss of life during the persecution.

Two days after D-Day he was with the first planes that landed on the newly captured airfield in Rangoon, and as soon as possible he made his way to Toungoo, and found Pastor Thara Myaing still there. By this time he was Major James Baldwin, and in his official capacity he was able to render the most valuable assistance to both workers and believers.

Referring to his visit to Toungoo, Pastor Tha Myaing wrote: "At last the short-legs (Japanese) have been driven out, and the long-legs (English) have come back. We rejoice because among the soldier missionaries of various denominations, there was also one of our church—Thara Baldwin. His superior officers have given him charge of the Karen troops' spiritual welfare, and the Karens small and great all respect him because he is patient and humble, and assists us in so many ways. The whole Karen nation is happy and loves him, and they enjoy his exhortations." After pleading for all the old Karen missionaries to come back quickly, Tha Myaing added this word of sorrow, "My wife is sleeping with those who await the second coming of the Lord, and my son, Saw Enoch, is no more. He lost his life while a member of the air force."

Our first regular missionary to re-enter Burma was Pastor A. J. Sargent. From his earliest letters I quote:

"Here I am in Burma, and what destruction I find everywhere. As our boat entered the Rangoon River, we looked about us for evidences of war but many of the ruins are al-

224

ready overgrown with jungle. Our approach to the dock section soon revealed that there were no docks. We looked for Rangoon, but could see only piles of rubble. The Sule Pagoda stuck up in the center like a sore thumb. Many sidewalks were overgrown with grass, and the streets were full of chuck holes. The officials of the Burma Government were quite nice and the colonel in charge of debarkation drove me in his own jeep to our people.

"I am living with Saya Deacon. For three days I have done nothing else but meet the believers as they came in. I had an open meeting with them yesterday.

They were all so happy that they were in tears. Of course their eyes were also on the boxes of clothing.

"They were desperate for clothes. In some of the villages the boys tell us the people clothed themselves with gunny sacking. And in other villages men were stationed at the entrance to warn strangers not to enter as the people were all naked. So after the meeting I opened the box. How pleased they were. With longyis (Burmese skirts) selling at Rs. 35 to Rs. 80 each, they felt themselves rich with two longyis and a shirt. It was January 1, 1946, and it all came as a wonderful New Year's present. Some of the workers are painfully thin and need food other than rice very badly.

"Perhaps they have suffered more than any other people in the world. All Christians were taken for spies and arrested for questioning. In order to make them talk, live electric wires were applied to their eyes, faces, and hands, and many of our own boys were tortured like this. They were beaten and cuffed and starved and some of them bayoneted to death long after they began wishing for death. On the least suspicion they were arrested and taken to jail. Some

15   225

ran away into the jungle, then the dacoits (robbers) got them. Thara Peter had lots of trouble. He was trading up and down the Salween River so that he could visit the church members.

"Now I know you want to know about Po Shwe and his companions who were murdered. It appears that the Burmese and the Karens started fighting, and Myaungmya was surrounded by Karens who were going to wipe out the Burmese; and the Burma National Army, composed of all sorts of jungle men, came to drive the Karens away, but were beaten off. They went to the Japanese, who sent officers, machine guns, and ammunition, so that the Karens, who were poorly armed, were driven off. Then came a time of bloody revenge. U Po Shwe and Daniel were out on a peace mission, trying to stop the fighting between the Karens and Burmese, and when they returned, they gathered about 28 of our people to their house, and there they stayed, but were soon betrayed by the people living around our compound. The Burmese came to U Po Shwe's house and arrested all of them. So all our people and hundreds of others were taken to the jail. Every morning the Burmese would call out twenty men, take them to a big grave, and bayonet them to death or cut off their heads with their swords. The prisoners in jail thought that those called out every morning were to be released, so when they were called they rushed toward the door to be among the twenty. The second day U Po Shwe was among the group, along with Saya Kan Bein, Po Be, Jan Se, and Po Ngwey. They took them to the big grave and bayoneted them to death. They say that Po Shwe got up out of the hole three times, but each time he was bayoneted and kicked back. So my best friend and wonderful Christian, trying to promote

226

peace as a preacher of Jesus, died for his Master. It is so sad and terrible that one can hardly think it possible. Burma seems empty without him.

"One day Sanchee pressed toward the door, thinking the twenty were going to be released. Then he rushed back to get something to take with him, and when he got back it was too late—the door had been closed. Next day he rushed forward, but went back to take his little brother with him, and was too late again. He did not know that the delay saved him.

"In the same jail Daniel pressed forward one day to be among the men called, and at the door the man who kept guard turned out to be one of his father's old policemen, and he whispered to him to go back. But Daniel tried again, and the man said, 'No, you must not go out, you do not know what you are doing. Go back, or they will kill you.' Then Daniel knew what they had done to Po Shwe, Po Ngwey, poor little Po Be, and his father and brother.

"Just about that time orders came from the Japs to stop killing; otherwise all the Karen women and children would have also perished. My heart aches for these people as they tell me how after the first shock, they spent ten days or two weeks singing and praying. Surely at the coming of Jesus these faithful men and women will wear a crown, and we shall meet them there.

"And so the stories came one after another, telling of suffering, starvation, and torture by electrically pulling off fingernails. I have been sitting and talking to these faithful boys and have wondered at their determination. Very few of them escaped persecution altogether. Two of Mr. Knight's boys were killed.

"However, comparatively few of our workers and believers lost their lives, though all our workers were forced to support themselves by working in the fields or as clerks or translators or traders. Prices of necessities went up terribly from ten to two hundred times the former price, so that oil was 100 rupees a *viss* [2.6 lbs.], a jacket 800 rupees, a common sun helmet, 250 rupees. [A pre-war rupee was worth 32 cents.]

"Rangoon was caught between the Burmese and Japanese, and was machine-gunned and bombed by the British as they came to the rescue. The city is badly destroyed. Our mission building is still occupied, but the church is free. The front door is wrenched off, and it is in bad repair. However, it escaped a great deal of the damage that came to other buildings.

"Our workers were so happy to see me that the boys put their arms around me and cried. They were so thin and pale. Saya Chit Maung's cheekbones almost pierced the skin of his face, and Tun Sein and Myat Kyaw were in a similar condition. Chit Maung has been the strong one, keeping so many together and shepherding them. He supported himself and others by his garden and paddy field, away off in the jungle. Also Thara Tha Myaing has gone his way through the jungle preaching, never resting, and is still out doing the same!

"The workers are all quite proud of the fact that they have been self-supporting, and declare that they have learned a lesson not to be so dependent on the mission in the future."

Before many days Elder Sargent was able to find Major Baldwin, and together they were able to make a tour, under guard, of our work in Upper Burma. It was found that the buildings of our training school at Meiktila had been so badly bombed that it would be impossible to open the training school there for the present. However, the buildings at our station at Myaungmya, where Po Shwe had been murdered, were still intact. The lights, the electric wiring, the fence, the water pipes, had all been stolen, but with some repair it was thought possible to reopen the Burma Union Mission training school at Myaungmya, and can you guess who was chosen to have this honor? Lenny Hare! Yes, the little boy born in Burma and reared beside the old haunted Pagoda of Ohn Daw.

He too had found some treasure of his own at Pacific Union College, and he and his brave wife Esther were among the next missionaries to arrive in Rangoon. With what rejoicing the teachers rallied to him. Repairs were quickly gotten underway, U Pu Nyo came as head master, and among the faculty members was Barnabus! Barnabus the son of Thara Peter! Barnabus who had played mud pies and motorcars with Lenny beside the old haunted pagoda! Within a few weeks the attendance of the training school reached 120, bringing new courage and cheer to the whole field.

Now let us turn to the Salween district and see what happened there. A letter from Peter, who was transferred to the Bassein district, not far from Myaungmya, written in his own style of English, says:

"Now, Thara, I like to inform you how I have been getting along through these four years period. In a brief note I like to state as follows: 1942 January the Kamamaung School had been closed down. One day Captain Seagraves came in, and said, all have to leave the place because the enemies were draw nigh. I sent my children to Thada-U, but I still remain here with my wife. On 22d of February soldiers throw grenade at Kaw-Keyet guard, just one mile away. Four times bombs sounded. My boy Stephen came back and said, Hurry up! the enemy is coming! He took my hand and pulled me, so I followed him. After pushing ourselves in the jungle, the bombing of our mission station sounded. As I looked back, the smoke came up. I told my wife and the others, poor Ohn Daw is burned. I hid myself two weeks. I went to Kamamaung Buddhist priest. I explained him about my trouble. He gave me a note and asked me to go down to Shwegoon and see the chief Thakin there. I went down there. They gave me a certificate. I came up to Kamamaung again to see our place. Nothing is left except ashes. The mission property and mine is all lost.

"So we came down here to Naungkaring emptyhanded. Our people here were so kind to us. In 1943 March, I went up to Lapota and baptized four there. In the same year a paratrooper named Peter came back from India. The Japanese officers were looking for him. It seemed that someone misunderstand, and they pointed them to me. So they arrested the whole family of us, took us to Shwegoon jail, and kept us there twelve days till they caught paratrooper Peter. In February, 1945, I went up to Tilaneh and baptized two. The same time the Japanese officers saw me there and arrested me again. They kept me two days in the Kamamaung guard. The same year in July they arrested me again because they said Christians were all spies. They took me here and there making many kinds of trouble for me. Some times they took me in the cave, sometimes put me in the pit. I thought that they would bury me alive. They did me that way until they surrendered.

"During these four years we added twenty-two members to our church. In 1943 October, six were baptized in

Naungkaring Lake and March, 1944, four were baptized in the Lay Pota River. The same year in the end of April ten were baptized in Naungkaring again. In February 1945 two more were baptized in the Tilaneh River. We gratefully thank God that He has been so kind to us and has been with us through these past four years. Last week Brother Sargent and Major Baldwin were with us here. They gave us good consolation."

Poor Ohn Daw! Poor Peter! The buildings all burned! The well stopped up! The coconut palms and the mango trees all twisted and scorched! But the gospel of Christ could not be burned! The gospel light was not put out! Listen! When Thara Peter was transferred to Bassein, Thara Chit Maung, another one of Ohn Daw's boys, was elected superintendent of the Tenasserim Mission. A temporary headquarters was established at Paan, right in the center of our constituency, and at the first general meeting of the Burma workers to be held after the reoccupation, August 18, 1946, Pastor Chit Maung made this report:

"Our Tenasserim Mission Field includes the whole division of Tenasserim in Burma, which extends from the Toungoo hills in the north, down to Victoria Point in the south, along the coast of Burma. Geographically it is very mountainous. As in the days during the dark ages, so our faithful workers and believers had to take refuge in the mountains and dense forests. The gestapo police of the Japanese army caused us great trouble and hardship. Some of our brethren were betrayed into the hands of the enemy as spies for the British Government, and were arrested and kept in custody. But, by the grace and mercy of our heavenly Father, none of them were killed. In spite of these hardships and difficulties, our people have been looking forward to the dawn of a new day, and for the revival of our work.

"Many of our young men were forced to join the labor corps of the Japanese army, and were sent to the malaria-infested areas. And owing to the lack of medicines and proper treatment, we lost three of our very faithful prospective workers. They had been the best students in Meiktila Training School.

"No doubt all the workers who have been in Burma, have learned about our local mission station and head-quarters, at Kamamaung. It has been well known to our people everywhere from the year 1915 up to the time of the Japanese occupation. Every building on this mission station was set on fire by the enemy early in the occupation. There is nothing left, with the exception of the parched, scorched, and twisted coconut palms and mango trees. The whole campus is covered with thick bushes and jungle. Not one single charred post of any building can be found. But huge bomb craters and enemy trenches are seen everywhere.

"During my first visit to our old Kamamaung Mission School campus, four workers accompanied me. It was last April, the hottest month of the year. Everyone was so sad to see that our own beloved school was in such a condition. Two of my companions wanted to set fire to the dry bushes and shrubs to clean the place. I advised them not to do so, for I was afraid there might be some castaway shells or bombs that would explode in the fire. But they kept on insisting, and kindled the fire. While the fire was burning in one place, I heard the explosion of some cartridges. I then shouted to them to come away and keep clear of the fire. They did not pay any attention, but went on. I warned them again and told them that it was truly very dangerous. Reluctantly they came back to me at the old gate. No sooner

232

had they arrived at my side than the whole place shook and quivered with a loud roar. It was the explosion of a bomb. It is indeed very sad to learn of such a tragedy and the fate which has befallen our old mission station of Kamamaung. Now let me give you a very brief review of the outstations.

"Lapota is situated about twenty miles northwest of Kamamaung. Here we have quite a strong community of our church members, about thirty in number. With their leader Thara Ohn Bwint, our evangelist, and some other faithful lay workers, this community stood faithfully during the time of trial and hardship. They have a good school. Its enrollment is more than fifty. There are quite a few candidates in their baptismal class, who will be baptized at the coming local annual meeting, which will be held next dry season. They have also definitely planned to build a small church which will be solely for religious and church services.

"There is another place where we have four families of our church members. It is about seven miles northeast of Kamamaung. Our village schoolteacher at this place had to flee for his life. But although our believers in this village were converted from very strong animism, I am glad to report that only a few of them wavered in their new Christian experience. At present the teacher has returned, and the school has been reopened, and the members have reconsecrated their lives for more and stronger work for the Lord.

"For the time being we have our Tenasserim local mission headquarters at Paan, a small town on the Salween River, about forty miles north of Moulmein. Our union committee also has voted that a good and suitable site be chosen in the vicinity of this town for our local mission central school. It is a suitable place, with better and more convenient transportation and communication than Kamamaung itself. This new location is accessible from all parts of our Tenasserim field. Our people in the district and villages, believers and outsiders as well, are pleading earnestly for this institution to be re-established. Many of them have promised to assist and even solicit contributions in rice toward this new institution.

"Eight miles north of this new headquarters there is a place where many of our old workers took refuge during the occupation. The Adventist church community of this place has been very faithful. They suffered much from the enemy. Two of our workers were forced to go around the country to search for spies. One woman believer sixty years of age was imprisoned for forty days and was almost starved to death. In spite of all this, our people have been firm and true to their principles. At present we have a good school there of sixty pupils, which is the largest one in our Tenasserim field. It has two teachers, one of whom is self-supporting.

"There are two more places in the Don Yin, or the paddy field, area which I should not omit in this report. Although Satan tried his best to put a stop to our work in this section of the field, our people have successfully gone through the gloomy days of the past. A few gave up from discouragement but were reconverted by the faithful ones. Our brother, Thara Kalle Paw, who came home from Siam on furlough, proved to be a great help to our people of Naungkaring.

"At Natkyun, twenty miles south of our headquarters, we have a very faithful group of believers. It is interesting to note that this little church was raised up by the effort of a

234

lay preacher a few years ago. We very much regret the death of our brother Thara Po Gyaw, which occurred on the 21st of July, 1946. He was then the teacher at Naungkaring.

"There is another place which I also would like to mention in this report. It is ten miles south of our headquarters, and on the banks of the Salween River. I feel very sympathetic with this group of our believers, because their village was frequented by dacoits and notorious people during and after the occupation. Among our believers there is a brother who has opened his own little private school and has become very influential among the animist Sabbathkeepers of the surrounding villages. These animists are a group of people who keep Saturday as their holy day, but the rest of their creed resembles that of the devil worshipers. As the leader of these people died some time ago, our brother has seized this opportunity to convince them of the truth. We pray that God will be with this brother and help him to bring in many souls.

"Shwenyaungbin is the last place to mention. This is the mission station established by Pastor H. Baird on the Toungoo hills, about three thousand feet above sea level, and twenty-one miles east of Toungoo city.

"My dear wife and I were with this group. We fled to the mountains and the rocks with the workers Thara Baw Dee, Au Chu, Ka Yai, and some of our believers. We built little huts and planted gardens in the remote crevices of the mountains, and God gave us our daily bread. Sometimes we were comfortable, sometimes we were troubled, sometimes we smiled, sometimes we cried, but we were sustained by the promise of God.

"It was hard enough on us who were older, but the

235

little children suffered worst, before our little huts were built and our gardens began to produce, hiding here a few days, and there a few days. There was not sufficient food, and no medicine at all. Thara Baw Dee's little baby girl sickened and died. Then Thara Ah Chu's little girl died. Then Phebe lost a little girl, Thara My Ni also, and Thara Ka Yai's little son died. My wife's mother died with malaria, but her father, dear old Thara Tha Myaing, although a very old man now, never rests. He is always out in the villages preaching the gospel. However, through those awful days God's blessing was upon us, as the dear old hymn says,

> "For I know whate'er befall me,
> Jesus doeth all things well."

"And you will be glad to know that all through these experiences our Sabbath school and church services in this district were never interrupted. The mission buildings were intact during the occupation, but when the Allied troops reoccupied the place, as a result of the blasts and concussion of the eight big guns stationed there, our buildings were greatly damaged.

"Our Tenasserim Mission is now operating eight village schools with ten teachers, three of whom are self-supporting. According to the last report of June 30, we had 238 pupils in our schools.

"You will remember that the Japanese retreated through our territory, and you can well imagine what the retreating enemy would do to the people here in Tenasserim. Prices of commodities rose high, and everyone had piles of Japanese paper money and yet could not spend much. An egg cost at least one or two hundred rupees and a duck or hen, one thousand or more. Even then you could not find enough things to buy. Our people have accumulated church offerings and tithes in this worthless currency which we cannot take into account. But let me report that our tithe which has come into our treasury since the reoccupation of the British troops, that is, from June, 1945, to June, 1946, excluding workers' tithes, is 894 rupees and three annas in Indian currency. This may mean a small amount to you, but not so to us here in Tenasserim, for I know our people suffered great loss at the hands of the enemy, and also at the hands of robbers.

"In closing, let me assure you we have greatly appreciated your sacrifice and gifts of clothing which we have lately received. We humbly solicit your interest and prayers, that the Lord may prosper our work here in this Tenasserim Mission field of Burma."

And so the story goes on. There can be no end to it till Jesus comes. We *will* pray for the work in Burma. We *will* look forward to the new day of progress that is dawning there. But I have to stop somewhere, or this book will never be printed, so I must close my story here.

How glorious have been the struggles between the forces of evil and the forces of righteousness in this land of the haunted pagoda! How sweet have been the prayers that have ascended from the people of God! How acceptable has been their sacrifice! How noble has been their faithfulness! How valuable this "special treasure"! (Malachi 3:17, margin.) It is "gold tried in the fire," for even today God regards the trial of His children's faith as "being much more precious than gold that perisheth, though it be tried with fire." 1 Peter 1:7. "And they shall be Mine, saith the Lord of hosts, in that day when I make up My jewels." Malachi 3:17.